ATOMIC SUSHI

ATOMIC SUSHI

NOTES FROM THE HEART OF JAPAN

SIMON MAY

ALMA BOOKS

ALMA BOOKS LTD
London House
243–253 Lower Mortlake Road
Richmond
Surrey TW9 2LL
United Kingdom
www.almabooks.com

Atomic Sushi first published in 2006 by Alma Books Limited
Copyright © Simon May, 2006

Simon May asserts his moral right to be identified as the author of this work in accordance with the Copyright, Designs and Patents Act 1988

Extracts on p. 44 reprinted by kind permission of Random House Inc.
Extracts on pp. 58-59 reprinted by kind permission of *The Daily Yomiuri*
Extract on p. 46 reprinted by kind permission of the WTO

This is a work of fiction. Names, characters, places and incidents either are the product of the author's imagination or are used fictitiously, and any resemblance to actual persons, living or dead, business establishments, events or locales is entirely coincidental.

Printed in Jordan by the Jordan National Press

ISBN-13: 978-1-84688-002-5
ISBN-10: 1-84688-002-5

ACKNOWLEDGEMENTS

I am greatly indebted to my many Japanese friends and professional colleagues who welcomed me to their country, to my brilliant editor Mike Stocks, from whom both the text and the author benefited immeasurably, to Alessandro Gallenzi and Elisabetta Minervini for championing this project with such imagination and verve, to Nicky Hoberman, and to Kimiko and Stephen Barber.

Contents

ATOMIC SUSHI

PREFACE

When I was unexpectedly invited to be a visiting professor of philosophy at Tokyo University, the training ground of Japan's post-War ruling class and an institution seldom penetrated by foreigners, my first thought was: "the sushi!" – a year of unlimited access to those glistening strips of the world's freshest fish draped over beguilingly tepid, gently vinegary, sticky rice…

The gastronomic glories on which I ended up spending around half of my generous professor's salary were indeed mind-blowing. And so, it turned out, was the powerful quirkiness of ordinary things in Japan: lying, hygiene, leisure, friendship, toilets, love, commuting, education, marriage, death, memory and forgetting.

My record of everyday life in this maverick economic superpower consists of anecdotes (interspersed with some short reflections) of encounters and friendships with the most diverse people: students, sushi masters, international businessmen, lonely wives, feckless husbands, kimono weavers, hairdressers, healers, underworld figures, teachers, Zen priests and, inevitably, bureaucrats. All of them, in their different ways, express the whimsical as well as the sinister

1

sides of this enigmatic nation, its great strengths as well as its dangerous weaknesses. And, through these individuals, Japan seems to teach some very personal lessons to the West: how to love, how to forget our hurts, how to accept fate with joy rather than resignation, how to die with dignity.

I decided early on to resist, as far as I could, Japan's ethereal traditions – the magical rock gardens, temple gongs, geishas and tea ceremonies – which are so far from today's reality, and generally of more interest to Westerners than to Japanese. Instead, I wanted to explore my surprising insider access to the living culture of Japan, access that I owed to Tokyo University – that nursery and bastion of the country's nightmarishly closed elite system, which has allowed in only a handful of foreigners in the last hundred years. I was apparently the first British professor of philosophy since 1882.

Japan matters. Economically, it is the world's number two power. Its population is 10% the size of China's, but its economy is nearly three times bigger. Its GDP is more than twice the size of Britain's and 70% larger than Germany's. Politically, Japan is a pivotal, if discreet, player in Asia and the world. Militarily, it has quietly amassed a huge arsenal. If and when it manages to throw off its obsessive bureaucratization of almost every aspect of life, it will regain the supreme confidence that it used to possess – that empowering, but also dangerous, confidence in its superiority over all other nations.

The Japanese are not "inscrutable". The myth of their inscrutability might meet a need, of both Westerners and Japanese, to find Japan too unique, too weird, to be comprehensible. But it is entirely wrong, for the simple reason that Japanese behaviour is largely governed by social rules that are remarkably decipherable and predictable. If anything, it is the West that is inscrutable: nations are far more difficult to fathom when millions of individuals are making autonomous choices, swayed by their own particular impulses.

Atomic Sushi is, therefore, a series of snapshots, not only of one of the world's most fascinating countries at a great moment of crisis and potential rebirth, but also of the challenge Japan presents to our self-understanding as Westerners. For, in many ways, travel is about learning how to return home afresh: about finding one's way back to oneself.

1

KᴀFKᴀ'ꜱ Nɪɢʜᴛᴍᴀʀᴇ

The academic New Year started on 1st April, International Fool's Day. One brilliant morning a few days later, the wind caressing and the sky a deep blue, I made my way to Tokyo University's Department of Philosophy as a new visiting professor. I found myself fondly, and perhaps a little vainly, imagining the rousing welcome I might be extended by my future colleagues and students, but what I actually encountered was more like a crash course in the nightmarish excesses of Japanese bureaucracy – that noose around the neck of the nation which the Japanese not only tolerate, but even seem to crave. For before I could be allowed to do anything so incidental to a professor's life as exchange ideas with colleagues and teach students and worry about the curriculum, it was my inviolable obligation to become a real person in the Japanese sense by compressing my life onto a bureaucrat's hard disk, gaining my virtual reality.

The administrators began by demanding that I sign a declaration promising to be a loyal and honourable servant of the Japanese State. Submitting to this demand immediately unleashed a torrent of further requests. Among other things, I needed health tests to certify that my body fluids were unobjectionable and my body solids in good order, a declaration from my landlady about my accommodation costs, a certificate proving that I had attended primary school, a document registering me as an alien, and a diagram to illustrate the exact route I intended to take when travelling from home to university, and then from university to home again.

I hastened to provide the last of these on the spot, in the naive hope of stemming the bureaucratic onslaught with a relentless display of loyal goodwill. Like most appeasement strategies, it was doomed to fail. Three officials bent over me, intently scrutinizing my efforts to produce the vital diagram. After a moment or two they started to confer. The tone was disapproving. Politely, but strictly, I was told that although the drawing of a single arrow was an appropriate method of depicting my train journey into central Tokyo, it certainly wouldn't suffice when it came to representing the walk from my house to the station; indeed, for such a purpose it became clear that a single arrow was not only inappropriate, but derisory. That part of the route would need to be more accurately drawn, and to scale, so that the exact spatial relations of the streets would be clear. I was advised to ask my landlady to provide this map, since a foreigner who had made the journey only once would be unable to achieve the necessary precision.

The matter of the health tests had been ongoing for several months. While still in London, I had received an email spelling out in detail what was required from me, from stomach and lung X-rays to blood, urine and faecal analyses. My local doctor had dispatched a clean bill of health to Tokyo long before I arrived, but the state-employed medical technicians who pored over it hadn't been fobbed off by his summary report. Now, on my first day in my new position, I was asked to submit to a battery of follow-up investigations: for example, I was to provide a sample of my stools for comprehensive chemical analysis. This sample, I was told, should be obtained by carefully scraping a turd along its entire length – "not just one centimetre, Dr May". We also came to a consensus that I would scrape the turd around its girth, at three equidistant points. I was supplied with a little coloured diagram that graphically illustrated the most effective way to undertake this complex operation, in which a smiling Teletubby-like figure deftly sampled something that looked like a withered brown banana with a device resembling the little plastic spoon on a tub of ice cream at the cinema. I burst out laughing, not just at the bureaucrats' pedantry, but also at the professor rendering all these technical instructions into English, who was looking steadily more tortured by the task. But it was no laughing matter, as I was firmly told by one of the administrators.

Once the matter of my stools had been dealt with, the officials turned to a subject of almost equal significance – my financial situation. It seemed that my first month's payment was, unfortunately, "very complicated, very difficult", because I had failed to register myself with the Faculty Office by the first day of the academic new year. I felt I'd had reasonable grounds for not turning up on that day, given that it had been a Saturday, and there would have been no access to the buildings, no colleagues to induct me, no students to teach, and no bureaucrats to make me real. Reality, however, was of marginal interest to the university administrators. The fact was, not to be registered with them on the day that the general academic year started was problematic financially, even if at that point I had no duties to perform. It meant that the necessary authorizations and paperwork couldn't be completed in time for payday on

17th April. Nor could I be paid my first month's salary as soon as the administrative difficulties had been surmounted, because payments could only be made on the 17th of each month. I would therefore have to wait until the 17th of May for my first payment.

Any financial exigencies this might have caused me were relieved by the resolution of another tricky aspect of my financial situation: my expenses. I was told that although my air fare to Japan would of course be refunded, a refund of my £24 taxi fare to Heathrow Airport in London was an impossibility and could not be permitted under any circumstances; the administrators were adamant that the rules for transportation of foreign professors were quite clear on this, and they appeared to have copious documentary evidence to back up their convictions. To rectify my financial loss, however, they proposed issuing me with £2,000. This £2,000 comprised "moving expenses", and moving expenses – unlike taxi fares – were there in black and white in their fat rule book on employing foreigners.

I tried to tell the officials that I hadn't incurred any moving expenses, since I was merely renting a furnished house for a year. And that I wasn't asking for an extra £2,000. Vaguely alarmed that I would be seen as a grasping opportunist, I protested that £2,000 to cover a £24 taxi fare seemed, well, on the steep side… But there was no arguing with the rules and regulations, and eventually I succumbed to them out of relief at having cleared another administrative hurdle, amazed but undeniably content to have made a profit of £1,976 on twenty minutes in a London cab.

Other demands followed, the most important of which was that I should order my *hanko* – a personal stamp that authorizes and dignifies one's signature on all official documents, for example when opening a bank account or simply when sending a letter through the university mail system. But even the *hanko*'s magic has only limited powers to overcome bureaucratic roadblocks. I quickly discovered that sending a letter through the university mailing system was merely one aspect of sending a letter through the university mailing system: the other aspect involved filling in, signing and stamping a special form that documented the existence of the letter, precisely when it was sent, and the correct identities of the sender and the recipient. It was somehow taken for granted that the physical artefact of the letter itself was insufficient grounds for assuming that the letter definitely existed.

All this left me in no doubt: the administrators of Tokyo University were my nemesis. Even before my arrival I had been inundated with emails for months, emails requesting arcane details of every stage of my life, from my first kindergarten frolics to the last gasps of my previous employment and beyond, and almost every piece of new information I supplied provoked a request for an official certificate to prove it was true. When I discovered that my primary school no longer existed, I was asked to present an official certificate to show that it had been "abolished". When I supplied the months in which I had probably entered and left it, I was told that I needed an official certificate that stated the exact dates. When I protested that I simply couldn't provide this, because there was no record of the dates and therefore recovery of such information was impossible, they requested a further official certificate stating that in Britain it is at times impossible to certify such information. And when I replied by pointing out that in Britain there is no certifying authority that exists for the purpose of certifying that something is impossible to certify, they asked me to state this with a certificate, certified by myself.

That I would have been unlikely to end up with a doc-torate in philosophy without successfully making it through kindergarten didn't strike the bureaucrats as relevant. Each step of my education and professional career required verification, and every time they encountered a procedure that differed from Japanese custom, they asked for an official certificate to explain it. Why were my degree certificates from Oxford University signed by someone called the "Assistant Registrar", rather than by the "President"? Did this mean that my degrees were faulty? I desperately tried to evade the request for another official certificate by saying that the signing of Oxford degree certificates by Registrars had probably gone on for centuries, and I made up a story about the "President" being too busy to sign thousands of certificates every year... but it was no good. They wanted a certificate – an official certificate – to certify that certificates from Oxford University were always signed by Registrars, even if this task was occasionally delegated to Assistant Registrars. It was requested that the certificate should be accompanied by a formal definition of the functions and responsibilities of Registrars, and that this definition should be signed by the "President". I replied that Oxford didn't have a President, only a Vice-Chancellor, and that he was much too busy to provide signed definitions of the functions and responsibilities of Registrars. This was a real mistake, for it provoked the obvious demand to explain why a paltry *Vice*-Chancellor was involved in all this; surely it should be the Chancellor of the university who is much too busy to provide signed definitions of the functions and responsibilities of Registrars? Once I had been administrated into a gently keening despair on any single issue, the stalemate was broken by another request for a certificate, if necessary signed by myself, to prove that what I was explaining was true.

This absurd flood of bureaucratic requests about turds, kindergartens and the certification of the uncertifiable, whose purpose was wholly impenetrable but certainly had nothing to do with educating the youth of Japan, had been cascading over me for eight months. Until my arrival in Tokyo, I had naively supposed that these ludicrous procedures concealed some meaningful purpose, such as to test my endurance, to probe my team spirit, or to verify the claims in my curriculum vitae. Surely, once the university had gained some confidence in firstly my material existence and then afterwards my basic integrity, the deluge would abate? I could not have been more misguided. Accommodation stimulated the bureaucrats' appetite rather than checked it.

Since 2004 halting attempts have been made to free Japan's public universities from the tyranny of government officials. Not before time. The administrators of Tokyo University, one of the country's most illustrious national institutions, represented officialdom run amok. Appointed by the Ministry of Education, they were unaccountable to, and uncontrollable by, the academics whom they supposedly served. The Byzantine formalities to which they were so fanatically loyal had remained largely unchanged since the nineteenth century, when they were imported from Bismarck's Germany, a country whose culture, temperament, and philosophy have extensive affinities with Japan, for good and ill. The pen-pushers who still fill so many Japanese institutions and corporations do not, of course, represent the cutting edge of Japanese culture – but nor are they merely a harmless throwback. They are emblematic of the massive resistance to change that besets Japan at all levels of society, which has delayed, if not paralysed, thoroughgoing social, economic and political reform for many years.

They were my welcome to Tokyo.

2

COMMUTING WITH MICHELIN MAN

Of the hundreds of trains that I took between Tokyo and my home in Kamakura, few were delayed by more than a minute or two. Other lines, however, could be more unpunctual, and some extensively so, not because they were cursed with worse management, but because of the *jumpers* – those unfortunates who had lost the relentless battle for a secure position within Japanese society and were intent on doing away with themselves.

Certain key spots on the network were particularly in fashion, so you could predict where the delays would be worst. A rush-hour suicide might hold up over a million commuters for two or three hours, though the rail companies are so efficient at dealing with the mess of bodies on the tracks that they often have the trains running sooner than that. "Service temporarily suspended" or "human accident on the line" is the official announcement; everyone knows that yet another overworked or unemployed salaryman has succumbed to the strain and leapt. Suicide is still the best exit from overwhelming shame – and the shame of losing your job or being unable to pay off your debts can wipe out your social status and self-respect at a stroke.

Aside from the jumpers, the aspect of Japanese commuting that is most striking to the foreign eye is the ubiquity of the comic book. Many adults, mainly men but increasingly women too, whether wan-looking junior clerks in their blue suits or silver-haired captains of industry in power grey or senior government officials wearing permanent airs of importance, are poring over *manga* as thick as *War and Peace*. They appear transfixed by the images of bikini-clad girls (some of them looking decidedly under-age) in provocative poses: girls being betrayed by their lovers, or ritually abused and humiliated, or abducted by aliens. Most *manga* characters are stuck in two basic emotions, shock and lust, and their lives seem strictly limited to domestic feuds, office romps and clandestine affairs. In the really hardcore material you can see young women being gang-raped by crazed-looking villains wielding swords, red-hot pokers, and other motley instruments of torture. The reserved and peaceful citizens perusing these sadistic tracts are flipping over the pages with the same nonchalance, the same relaxed curiosity, as the other passengers with their newspapers and books and corporate reports, whiling away the long commute home.

Many Japanese tell you that *manga* are "safety valves" for brutal impulses, or that they're "works of art"; others decry them as perverse and corrupting. But whatever one's view, this immense appetite for *manga* reflects the powerfully erotic, sado-masochistic and violent fantasies that lie just below the surface of this extraordinarily ordered and subtle nation – fantasies to be found, perhaps, in all countries, but seldom so violently repressed in some contexts, and openly expressed in others, as in Japan.

Whatever reading material the commuters around me opted for, their favourite pastime was clearly not reading but being unconscious. Most people, from schoolchildren to senior citizens, are napping. Even in the morning rush hour, when the majority of passengers scarcely have enough room to stand on one leg, and when each packed carriage resembles a mass game of twister or some improbable species of human installation art, people sleep. It's quite common for your neighbour's head to dip gently onto your shoulder, for their back to slump against your chest, or indeed – if you're fortunate enough to be sitting down – for their whole body to collapse across your lap, as though such intimacy is a natural courtesy among passengers. Although the general rule in this society is that touching a stranger is a taboo loaded with impropriety and menace, on the trains such abrupt physical contact isn't found odd at all – unless, of course, one of the parties is a foreigner, in which case the taboo applies with double force. To be collapsed over an unknown foreigner's lap would be among the most embarrassing and even repulsive situations that any Japanese commuter could experience.

I remember one late-evening trip back to Kamakura – it was ten o'clock and the rush hour was still in full swing – when a very beautiful girl entered the packed train and stood in front of my neighbour, a clean-cut man probably in his early thirties. He was avidly reading the annual report of the Michelin tyre company, while picking from a packet of walnuts on which the manufacturer had announced, in English: WE PROUDLY PRESENT YOU OUR NUTS. PLEASE ENJOY THEIR CHEWINESS. He was riveted by the document and missed this unmissable new arrival. The girl wrapped her lovely fingers around an overhead handrail and immediately started dozing. Her head fell abruptly forwards, and her long luxuriant hair swept down in a glossy arc, brushing the top of the Michelin report and partially covering the enticing slogan on the front of her T-shirt: "COME NOW!" (When she later left our carriage, I was disappointed to discover that this delightful summons referred to nothing more raunchy than "WORLD WIDE PEACE", which was printed on the back.) As the train gathered speed, her body began swaying to and fro, her long, graceful legs rubbing enviably against my neighbour's knees. He was still impervious, rapt in a concentration deeper than that of the raciest *manga* reader. Every so often she lurched sharply backwards, bosom quivering in synch with the vibrations of the train, but her hand continued to grip the rail and she remained upright. Then she would bang forwards against him, her milky-white cleavage charmingly assaulting his face and the smooth skin of her leg rubbing along the inside of his. Mastering the finer details of the Michelin annual report must have been critical to keeping his job or to gaining a promotion that his family, friends and colleagues all expected of him; nothing except the threat of imminent social or economic death could begin to explain this man's superhuman composure.

Unfortunately for me, the train refused to jolt around in such a way that, for once, I would be the lucky one to be assaulted. With each impact, the goddess half-opened her eyes; her dilated pupils, drunk with tiredness or alcohol or something harder to fathom, seemed almost deranged, her unfocused expression alluringly wild. At one point her umbrella clattered to the floor and she dimly awoke, staring at it long and hard as though it were some artefact from a distant world... then she succumbed to sleep again even as three of us, eager to touch her, however superficially, competed to pick it up and hook it back onto her delicate arm. Meanwhile Michelin man continued to pore over his profit-and-loss statements with an intensity that is usually confined to starving lions when stalking fat and wayward antelopes. And then, as the train approached a station and came to a stop, she opened her eyes, looked briskly around, exited elegantly and stepped deftly onto an escalator. She passed out of view, a clutch of regretful men watching her go, as a heroic commuter turned his attention to *Debt-to-Equity Ratios in the European Automotive Sector*.

I never got used to the talent of Japanese commuters for keeping track of exactly where they are even while slumped asleep in a seat or hanging comatose from a handrail. They can will themselves from the sleeping to the waking state in a split second, striding off the train and down the platform in full self-possession. This subliminal attentiveness speaks of something very deep in their nature: a pervasive and acute alertness to their environment and its most subtle signals, instilled perhaps by their constant vulnerability to earthquakes, which can strike day or night without warning. Such alertness and subtlety are part of their virile realism, deserting them only when fashion or group hysteria or unthinking devotion to duty gets the better of them – as history shows it can.

Perhaps Michelin man was so hopelessly devoted to his duty that he had been deserted by his own virile realism – and all the while the loveliest reality was in front of him, if only he'd cared to look up and see.

3

The Rat and the Sushi Master

"The Ayatollah", as I nicknamed the elderly sushi master on account of his forbidding air of spiritual authority, understandably preferred not to have foreigners in his restaurant. They would compromise the purity of his calling, quite apart from their uncouth tendency to behave as if they had rights – the right to see a menu or a price list, for example, or the right to choose what to eat. At first, he refused point-blank my requests for reservations, even when I arranged for a Japanese colleague from the University to telephone on my behalf. After a few weeks, though still refusing to address me directly, he granted me a reservation "provided the foreigner is accompanied by a Japanese". Finally, I attained the Holy Grail: admission on my own. A month after that he extended to me, for the first time, what looked like a smile – a grim, melancholy compression of the lips that signalled my conditional acceptance as an acolyte of his sect. Eventually, his counter became my refuge most Tuesday evenings after lectures.

He was an imposing figure: gaunt, fearfully impassive, minimalist in his gestures. He communicated almost wordlessly with his two assistants and barely at all with the even lower forms of life who toiled in the kitchen. His commands – say, for pickles or a special cut of fish – were instantly relayed down the hierarchy, and the responses were transmitted back up the same pathway.

The quality of the sushi was mind-blowing: none I'd had in the West came close. Of course, it wasn't cheap: in the evening you couldn't get away with under $200 per head, not including sake. Extras of fatty tuna came in at $30 a piece. In the gastronomic paradise that is Japan, you quickly find a whole new meaning to the phrase "putting your money where your mouth is".

The authority of the Ayatollah was not to be under-estimated. His confidence in his own position, the prestige invested in him by the conservative theology of his art, his perfect composure and coordination, his decades in command of his temple of gastronomy, made any subversion of the ruling order – especially one involving a foreigner – impossible to imagine. The idea of him seriously losing face, of his hands shaking with nerves, of his staff running around like headless chickens, was all but unthinkable. But one day it did happen.

"What's that?" I blurted, hardly able to believe what I was seeing as I was about to place another piece of arkshell sushi into my mouth.

Nobody said anything, but the master and his staff had seen exactly the same thing as I had seen, and they were temporarily paralysed. A large rat, overfed on the world's freshest, choicest and most exquisitely prepared fish, had sprung off a kitchen table directly into the restaurant, and was scurrying at speed past the feet of the diners.

"Look!" I called, open-mouthed, gaping at where the bloated rodent disappeared into the shadows. "Did you see that?"

"No," answered the senior assistant.

The master himself was silent and unmoving.

"That was a rat!" I gasped, instantly losing my usually insatiable appetite for sushi.

"A big mouse," the assistant said hopefully, and next to him the master's stern grimace softened into a queasy smile.

"No, no," I insisted, disgusted by the sight of the ugly beast that might have been foraging on all our dinners, "definitely a rat!"

The Ayatollah's formidable façade was slipping; he fumbled with my sea-urchin sushi, and the rice crumbled and fell between his fingers. His staff, distressed by such fallibility in their master, didn't know where to put themselves. The two middle-aged waitresses in kimonos started searching discreetly for the missing creature, their faces lined with controlled worry. The other customers at the counter dutifully carried on their after-work rituals of corporate loyalty, too involved in their bantering, or too drunk, to notice the desecrator in their midst.

"Don't tell them!" the master's other assistant hissed politely under his breath, indicating my neighbours with a tilt of his head and smiling obsequiously at me. One of the waitresses, still unable to track down the rat, echoed his request with a seductive, beseeching gaze that said, "You are an insider here now; please don't break ranks."

The master had retired to a murky region of the kitchen to lick his wounds. Seeing that his humiliation was being successfully delegated to his staff, and perhaps remembering his hallowed position, he was slowly regaining his confidence and gearing up to punish me for witnessing the rat. His instrument of punishment turned out to be the bill.

$340 was the price of my miserably truncated meal, much more than I had ever been charged there before, even for the most indulgent feasts. As in most good sushi bars, there was no menu or price list, the bill depending on a combination of the master's mood, the cost of the ingredients he decided to allow you to try and, above all, his respect for you. In the respect stakes – which were essentially determined by your loyalty and your capacity to appreciate his art – I had been making solid progress. I ate with my eyes closed for particular delicacies, I refused sea urchin unless it was from Hokkaido, I knew to reorder only the freshest courses, I showed the right combination of humility and confidence towards the master, I always dunked only one end of the sushi, fish downwards, into the soy sauce (rather than soaking the whole piece in it, as most *gaigin* and many Japanese do), I learned to rattle off the Japanese names for the most exotic fish, and I avoided bringing people like Western investment bankers into his temple, who tried to pay with credit cards and believed such philistine absurdities as "the customer is king"…

In the Ayatollah's eyes, these were considerable achievements for a Westerner, and he had rewarded them over time with a steadily diminishing bill, no matter what I ate. But the rat changed everything. I, a foreigner, had witnessed a chink in his authority. Normality, and therefore norms, had been blown away. Reservations once again became too "complicated" to secure, and even offering to go there with a Japanese couldn't restore me to grace. I was never permitted to return.

4

The Mega-Corporation and the EU Spy

The mega-corporations of Japan are not noted for scouring the common rooms of the Academy for Western Professors of Philosophy to install on their boards of directors. But a couple of months after I arrived in Japan I was invited to the headquarters of one of these great organizations. It seemed that they were planning a new investment fund for Europe, and were thinking of interviewing me for a gratifyingly lucrative position on the Fund's international board. A combination of curiosity and aversion to looking a gift horse in the mouth made it hard not to go along for the ride, and so I agreed to attend a preliminary meeting where they could find out more about me.

I was escorted to the seventeenth floor of a gleaming new building and straight into a large boardroom, where several middle-ranking functionaries were dutifully waiting for me. Their demeanours were pristine; their bland stares gave nothing away that hadn't been pre-cleared with a superior; and they evinced that perfect self-censorship that can make each Japanese his or her own oppressor, so that the whole country resembles a dictatorship without a dictator.

The boardroom was smart, but low-key and functional by Madison Avenue or Mayfair standards. I small-talked cautiously with my cohort of hosts, though the unspoken thought on all our minds was that the head honcho hadn't shown up on time. Nor did he show up soon afterwards; and since only small talk was permissible before his arrival, we were forced to grope around for more banalities, steadily running out of things to say about the cherry blossom season, whether Westerners could stomach raw fish, and the splendid views of the Imperial Palace, which could be seen in the distance, half-hidden within its extensive gardens.

The lateness of the senior figure was starting to make his subordinates very uneasy. It was a bad omen, a signal that – for whatever random reason or emphatic decision or twist of fate – I wasn't after all a serious candidate for a position on the board of the mega-corporation's European Fund. As we floundered in the shallowest outer reaches of conversational desolation, I realized that through no fault or action of my own I was being transformed from a respected guest into a thundering embarrassment. The discomfort on their faces suggested that there were no rules on how to deal with thundering embarrassments who had somehow made their way into the executive suite on the seventeenth floor.

Eventually the Managing Director arrived. He was polite, professional and distant. To some extent his presence restored credibility to my position. Now I felt that I was in the sort of Japanese environment that is most familiar to Westerners: the tough, no-nonsense, well-organized world of big business. After we had worked our way through a shortlist of the usual pleasantries – he was senior enough to shortcut the more vacuous ones and to dispense briskly with the rest – the grilling began. At first his questions were about the precise content of every job I had ever held, how these jobs cohered with one another, and how my education had prepared me for them – a laundry list more or less identical to Tokyo University's. But after a while he went deeper, asking about motives: why did I apply for a particular job? Why had I moved on? Why had I accepted the Tokyo University professorship? Once these matters had been dealt with to his satisfaction, and without a change in tone or a blink, without the slightest indication that his questions were about to take on a different aspect, he calmly and in all seriousness asked me if I was a spy.

"Sorry?"

"Are you a spy?"

"No!"

"You don't belong to the European Union's espionage service?"

"Of course not. As far as I know, they don't have one anyway."

I stared at him, baffled, trying to suppress a snigger or two – the idea that the EU could successfully run its own espionage service would bring tears of laughter to the most ardent Europhile. But the questions were insulting too – from where had he cobbled up such anxieties?

"So, Dr May, you're not a player in the international arms industry?"

"What?"

"Let me be a little direct: are you really in Japan in order to deal in weapons?"

If I'd had the special key required to call the lift to the executive floor, I'd have walked out. Instead, I asked him to explain.

"Your CV, Dr May…"

"Sorry, I'm not sure I understand you."

Running his finger over a line on the page – I strained to make out which one from the other side of the large boardroom table – he turned to one of his colleagues and started conferring inaudibly. I was beginning to feel rattled, mainly by his condescending tone – the sort that is quietly confident of the other's mendacity, while pretending that the accused is innocent until proved guilty. And yet his insinuation held a hilarious fascination to it, and I was eager for him to get to the nitty-gritty. He got there at last: on my list of publications was an incriminating book I'd co-authored. With laboured precision, he read out the title to all present, as though it sufficed to indict me:

"*The European Arms Market and Procurement Cooperation.*"

Looking up at me gravely, as if all that remained were for me to confess my crime and hold up my wrists for handcuffing, he added:

"Why would anyone write *that* book if he isn't working for weapons manufacturers or the secret service? We really don't understand this, Dr May."

I was oddly flattered. No one had invested this obscure first book of mine with such significance before; an out-of-print work that only a few academics had noticed was provoking controversy at the highest levels of corporate Japan. But while my eyebrows were still up and my mind searching for an explanation that wouldn't inadvertently stoke his suspicions, he leant forwards, rather urgently, and unleashed his main objection:

"If you join the Board, won't you try to influence the Fund to invest in the arms industry? Which it is forbidden to do!"

"I don't know anybody in the arms industry. I'm not interested in it. The book was just…" But it was more or less useless trying to explain my position from the other side of the chasm of cultural assumptions that separated us: he saw my early scribblings as hastening Armageddon, perhaps even intentionally, whereas to me they had been a tentative step up the academic ladder. I did my best, however, to explain that I had been a commentator on such matters, not a participant. I talked about the highly political nature of arms procurement in Europe, the enormous waste of taxpayers' money that props up the flagship arms companies of the Western nations, and the inherent corruption of cosy relationships between big companies and governments (something that mega-corporations in Japan happen to know a fair bit about). I sought to convince him that when it comes to international espionage and the sale of high-tech arms consignments, I had failed to clock up the achievements he was so eager to credit me with.

The longer our exchange went on, the more it became bogged down in misunderstanding. The head honcho was feeling frustrated by his inability to flush out the suspicious activities he was sure my book must be concealing, and I was once again feeling like an embarrassment to his organization.

At least the experience gained me some insights into the Japanese. First, over half a century after the end of World War Two, it is still hard to overstate their sensitivity to weapons and war. The defeat of militarism in 1945 effected a massive and, in great part, genuine about-turn of the national mentality. Overnight the welfare state replaced the warfare state. For many, even the *word* "military" is sordid, to be uttered only in hushed tones, and then with the caveat that Japanese forces (actually among the largest and best equipped in the world) are for "self-defence" only. Though some feel humiliated by this taboo, especially ambitious populist politicians who wax liberally about discarding it, the shackles of absolute defeat are going to be hard to throw off for a long time yet.

Second, the Japanese like a good conspiracy theory – a trait not unrelated to their deep predilection for superstition. They are a society in which rumour and gossip and intrigue are everywhere. This is obvious in any big institution, which will be rife with backstabbing and bitching, with cliques that can decide one's destiny with arbitrary admittances and summary expulsions.

Third, they can flip from uncritical acceptance to intense mistrust in a moment. Like the proverbial butterfly whose flapping wings trigger a distant hurricane via a cascade of small events, some minor or unfounded suspicion can precipitate one's downfall. Relationships will be exceptionally stable if both sides act with unshakeable predictability, but the slightest deviation from normal behaviour can arouse the most fantastic misgivings. Given the national pastime of denial and secrecy, any reputations tarnished by such misunderstanding can be nearly impossible to restore.

My unnerving dialogue with a senior figure of a mega-corporation was really only a function of these three national traits. I doubt that I ever managed to wriggle free of his assumption that I was an arms-toting secret agent, and so in the end I wasn't surprised that this five-figure non-executive directorship – that would have paid for so much great Japanese food – was never mentioned again.

5

Finding the Three S's

The Managing Director of the mega-corporation was a powerful man. But there are powerful men in Japan, and then there are men so powerful that they operate like gods within their own universes. Mr Ryoichi Sasagawa – whom I had met nineteen years before after entering an international essay competition for young people – had been one such man. In fact I might never have upped sticks and moved to Japan for a year if it weren't for that essay competition, organized by the Japanese Foreign Ministry in the Eighties. The title of the essay was something like: 'How can Japan and Europe cooperate to create global peace?' These days I feel that this would be a tough one to crack, but when I was twenty-five years old the solution to this important question seemed well within grasp. So, first taking the precaution to check where Japan was on the map, I raced to my local library and concocted a compendium of clichés sufficiently upbeat to secure the pride of a young man and the approval of a panel of politically correct bureaucrats. To my delight, I won one of the prizes, an all-expenses-paid junket to Japan.

The official schedule seemed designed to confirm every foreigner's preconception of Japan as an economic superpower dotted with temples, geishas, besuited salarymen and obedient wives. After a few days I started longing for something unexpected. We had toured immaculate car factories, met workers singing songs in praise of their companies, "done" ancient Kyoto and listened to lectures from earnest professors about how the Japanese brain, unlike its cruder Western counterpart, has no problem believing that things can be both good and bad or true and false at the same time.

The hospitality was also unstinting. On arrival I was handed a little brown envelope stuffed with freshly printed Yen bills, delightfully crisp and smooth to the touch. Prepaid meals and hotels awaited me at every stop, and no meeting began without a gift-giving ceremony. It seemed ungrateful, but all this organization was getting me down. I felt throttled by the lack of free-flowing conversation. Jokey exchanges were formulaic. Even spontaneity was choreographed. Instead of the famous three S's of Japan – Silence, Smile and Sleep – I hoped for Scandal, Salaciousness and Sex.

Mr Sasagawa was the answer – the megalomaniac elderly billionaire capo of a vast speedboat-racing empire, plus Class-A war-crimes suspect to boot. Only a young person with ample naivety and cheek would send a letter to such a figure requesting a meeting, just on the off-chance that he might say yes. So, taking advantage of my new-found position as a temporary ambassador for friendly international relations, I wrote to him about my urgent desire to explore his views on world peace; in reality I just wanted to meet the man because his life was one of extraordinary risk, drive and success. It was said that his economic ambitions, though not his methods, mirrored those of post-war Japan.

Mr Sasagawa responded favourably to my impudent suggestion. Not only did he say yes, but he sent a bus-length white limousine to fetch me from my hotel. Sitting in that limousine, prodding its mysterious buttons and levers and devices, stroking its furs and leathers, seeing my satisfied reflection gazing back at me from polished woods, I became fully convinced of the fabled power and glamour of Mr Sasagawa. I enjoyed the thought that a man reputed to be so dangerous could create wealth of such reassuring safety.

I was whisked through Tokyo's traffic to a smart building near the city centre, then down into an underground parking lot, where I was deposited in a gleaming lift which launched me upwards hundreds of feet to the Presidential penthouse at the top. The lift doors opened onto a cavernous office, which I peered into gingerly, like a bird that has to be prodded out of its cage.

It rapidly became evident that there was something of the James Bond villain to Mr Sasagawa's sense of style: two ineffably beautiful girls in tiny miniskirts were waiting for me. They greeted me with flawless English and ushered me towards a huge armchair where I was to await the great man; at the time, it seemed entirely natural that the seat they'd shown me to was placed between a pair of stuffed tigers, their mouths frozen into eternal snarls.

Moments later, Mr Sasagawa entered through a side door. Modestly dressed in the Japanese businessman's identikit suit, his small, compact figure was dwarfed by the leggy beauties who rushed over to flank him. Like many hugely rich Japanese, he didn't like his personal appearance to exude wealth, and his neat, down-to-earth look seemed all the more impressive for the opulence of his office.

He walked briskly towards me, measured up my insignificance with some surprise, and grunted – which one of the girls translated as "Mr Sasagawa invites you to sit down please".

"What can I do for you?" he asked indifferently, probably expecting me not to waste a moment before asking him for money, and perhaps toying with the idea of giving me some, if only to get our meeting over with. He seemed puzzled by my presence, and his eyes darted around restlessly – as if searching out a more impressive visitor.

"I'd like your views on world peace," I said absurdly, realizing that I ought to have concocted a slightly more specific agenda. "Young people," I stammered, "Britain, Europe, should do more to create international order. Together. With Japan. How can we achieve this?"

His subdued irritation at having allowed such a low form of life into his crowded schedule gave way to a strident monologue, peppered with allusions to his own efforts to create a world of love and understanding. Cold, mercurial, and with a menacing aura, he paused between each staccato pronouncement as his translator politely rendered it into impeccable English.

"It is the responsibility of your generation to create world peace," he informed me, adding, "*my* generation has done all it can."

"I see…"

"Japan is too dependent on the United States," he barked, as the miniskirted beauties raced to transcribe their master's maxims. "Europe should complete the triangle of peace."

I had done a little bit of research into the great man. He apparently spoke of himself as "the world's richest fascist". It was said that he had made his first fortune by assassinating the chiefs of mineral-rich cities in China, and then plundering their wealth, including the wealth derived from narcotics dealing. It seemed an unusual apprenticeship for building world peace, but I didn't get much of a chance to disagree with what he said, and certainly wouldn't have risked anything so forthright.

The interesting part of Mr Sasagawa's view of the world was not the call for universal brotherhood, which you hear in Japan over and over again. Instead it was his conspiracy view of history: things happen only because small cabals plot them. You can never trust what people say, but have to look behind it for their real motives, which are usually base and self-interested. You must watch like a hawk for the omens and signs that betray those motives. And once you know what you want, you should say and do whatever it takes to succeed.

Mr Sasagawa insisted that the only cabal that counts in today's world is the West, led by the United States. In order to be in on it, Japan needed to avoid any repetition of its militaristic past. This meant talking peace and carrying a big wallet – a strategy that seemed to have paid off handsomely for Sasagawa, judging by the pictures of world leaders that graced his room, many of them signed with personal statements of admiration and gratitude.

After fifteen minutes, Mr Sasagawa stopped speaking and abruptly declared that the meeting was over. While I floundered between the two stuffed tigers, wondering about the protocol of getting from the armchair to the lift, he signalled to a flunky, who at once rushed over to me and presented me with a gift. Then Sasagawa stood up and personally herded me to the lift at a sharp clip. Just as the doors were about to close he further disempowered me by asking a last-minute question. By the time the question had been interpreted, I had nearly disappeared, peering at him as I was from between a crack in the doors. Assistants scrambled to wrench the doors open, so that I could benefit from his final pearl of wisdom:

"Can you," Mr Sasagawa said, "can you run up the stairs of the building to the penthouse without getting out of breath? Because I can, in my eighties, and that is the secret of my success! Relentless training," he barked, as the doors glided shut once more; "Discipline!" he added at the last moment. Then he and his beautiful assistants vanished, and I was alone in the lift, plummeting back down to my lowlier level in life.

In the limo going back to the hotel, I resisted my overwhelming desire to open the present. It was only in the privacy of my room that I tore into the expensive layers of wrapping paper, to find that Mr Sasagawa had given me a clock. The clock was designed around a picture of Mr Sasagawa. The picture showed him bearing his elderly mother on his back and carrying her up a hill. On the hour, every hour, this striking image of Mr Sasagawa's filial piety lit up inspirationally.

I have no plans to bear my own mother on my back and carry her up a hill; surely it was enough just to give her the clock. It still stands today in her kitchen, should she feel a pressing need to reflect on her son's youthful investigations into world peace. But the picture stopped lighting up some time ago, and Mr Sasagawa is dead.

6

FLYING GOLDFISH

A goldfish shooting out of a girl's vagina some eight metres; a $400 bar bill for two whiskeys; a high-tech toilet going on the rampage: many of the world's most surprising surprises are in Japan.

I had been invited to the sprawling volcanic spa of Atami, near Tokyo, by Masamichi, an architect. He was a sinewy, humorous man in his mid-fifties who prided himself on a straight-talking style and an insatiable libido. This package of decisiveness and debauchery was his official trademark. He could be unflinchingly generous, and he belied the cliché that the Japanese are lacking in empathy, especially with foreigners. Masamichi understood people's strengths and weaknesses intuitively, and it was rewarding to experience Japanese culture in his perceptive company. He epitomized Japanese hospitality: that expert and unintrusive art of pampering the senses, performed against a background buzz of undemanding conversation and light banter. Not that such hospitality is always easy to experience. Guardians of consensus, order and silence, the Japanese often see talk as superfluous at best and vulgar at worst – an activity that conceals reality rather than reveals it. I'm sure there is a lot to be said for this reticence, but that doesn't make it any easier to endure the feelings of rudderless boredom it can leave you with.

There was nothing reticent about the girl with the super-charged vagina, however, to whom Masamichi's hospitality had led me. Nor, apparently, was there anything particularly smutty about her antics. It was good, clean fun for the few dozen men and women cheering her on in the "amusement" parlour. I arrived just as she was strangling a chicken with her twat. Extracting its limp head, she tossed the stunned bird to one side and replaced it with a long corkscrew already attached to a bottle of wine – the normal handle having been substituted for a round wooden ball as an understandable concession to comfort. Slowly – painfully slowly, it seemed – she pulled the cork out of the bottle and gaily offered a glass of wine to a gratified husband in the first row, to the great amusement of his wife. Then, the goldfish... With a flourish of her fingers she scooped it from a glass bowl and stuffed the writhing creature into herself, tail first. She stood on the stage, motionless, as silence closed in around her, staring defiantly downwards as if daring the fish to escape – then flipped onto her back, jacked up her pelvis, and sent her hapless prisoner not merely flying across the room, but plumb into a bucket of water near the entrance. The audience went wild. She got a standing ovation, and even the fish got a warm round of applause.

I wanted to stay and see what other feats a well-trained vagina can perform, but Masamichi insisted on taking me drinking.

The bars are where weary salarymen retreat to after their long days so that they can prove their corporate loyalty, make deals, and postpone going home to their wives. You can really get the feel for a neighbourhood by spending an hour in a typical bar after nine or ten at night, as you sit hip to hip with disillusioned middle-aged toilers and work your way through unusual sakes and foodstuffs. But Masamichi didn't want to take me to a typical local bar; he wanted to take me to the The Lead Cashew.

The Lead Cashew? Only when we arrived there did I realize that this intriguing pub name was Masamichi's attempt to pronounce "The Red Castle" – a dreadful dungeon of boredom sporting a proud boast over its entrance: "EXCLUSIVE, FOR GENTLE MAN!"

Only a foreigner would be stupid enough to try ordering Japanese drinks or food here. A basement room, it was decked out in plush velvet sofas and marble-topped tables with damask cloths, crystal glasses, gold-rimmed coasters and other signifiers of affluence. Groups of men sat around guffawing vehemently as pretty, alienated-looking hostesses – mostly students from China – deployed their nubile charms amongst greying egos. The girls twittered their lines and compliments ("Your eyes are so cute!") while their clients flirted benevolently. There were roles to be fulfilled in this place, and personal identities to leave behind for a few hours, and both the hostesses and the clients were dutifully doing their bit. Only those tables with particularly beautiful hostesses seemed to have an air of excitement about them: there the clients' faces glowed with the reflected purple-pink of the velvet sofas; smooth male hands sought every opportunity to stray across expanses of bare thigh; fresh bottles of whiskey and gin were ordered heedless of the astronomical mark-up.

The *mama-san* – the presiding hostess, a hard-eyed middle-aged lady with hair sculpted out of black glass – sat down at our table and fired a stream of thought-provoking questions at me while on autopilot.

"*Sensei* (teacher), how is it possible to combine the realms of thought and sex?"

"Thought can be a form of sex," I replied gamely. "Anyway that's what Plato said, and he was the founder of Western thought."

"O, ho, how so?" she giggled.

"Sex is union with another person, and thought is union with the world."

"Sex is more fun," she exclaimed. "Except it gets boring with one person!"

"Well, with thought," I said, "with thought you can have as many partners as you want, sometimes together."

"Oh, philosophers have such a strange sense of humour!" she quipped, affecting interest in our repartee as she went through the motions of esteeming and pampering me; but the rules of the game prohibited real engagement, just as they more or less prohibited real girls. The moment a conversation found its bearings, she would steer it back into no man's land. Her zeal was really reserved for optimizing her cash flow by filling up her clients' glasses as often as possible, and by redeploying her prettiest girls to the most well-heeled tables. She certainly showed her mettle when it came to hitting Masamichi with the bill for our drinks. All I could see of their negotiation, which was conducted discreetly by a little counter near the entrance, was their two heads locked in combat for an agonizing quarter of an hour; then Masamichi returned to our table, pale and resigned. $400 for two whiskeys... As far as I was concerned, anything that purchased our release was cheap at the price, so we beat as dignified a retreat as we could – escorted to the street, as is the polite custom, by the extortionate *mama-san* and the girls she had assigned to us. As I looked back, I saw the trio still standing at the threshold of the building, frozen into low bows until we turned the corner and disappeared out of their sight.

The appeal of Japanese clubs and bars is not easy to fathom, but their tedium and unpleasantness seem to be directly proportional to how expensive they are. Expensive means prestigious, and prestigious means popular. Of course, it's strangely true the world over that people will clamour for admission to haunts of all sorts if they know they're guaranteed to be ripped off, but in Japan this curious dynamic is supreme. I recall one particularly tedious club in the fashionable Ginza district of Tokyo where three glasses of whiskey and some bad Chinese wine cost my host $1,400; that is so expensive as to be very prestigious indeed, so the waiting list for membership of this club was over two years. But there are institutions which are even more prestigious than this: the Golf Clubs and the Rotary Clubs of Japan.

Nothing genuinely Japanese is permitted to occur within these deadly and highly prized places, unless you count an insatiable desire to emulate all things non-Japanese. And Chairman Mao's China didn't enforce a more rigid dress code than the regulation clothing, a patchwork of designer labels from Paris and Milan. As for the furniture and fittings, it is compulsory that everything is mock Regency and Belle Époque, while anything that isn't made out of marble is made out of mahogany. When it comes to the grateful members of these hellholes, their single objective is to create the impression of being the ultimate insiders. Such an impression is invaluable to businessmen on the long haul to a deal, which is why getting thoroughly milked in the Golf Clubs and Rotary Clubs of Japan is merely part of the job. Naturally the host will incorporate the expense of his ritual fleecing into his client's contract, so ultimately there is a little method to the madness.

Method and madness brings us to the Japanese toilet, and to Masamichi once more. During our evening of getting ripped off together in one dive after another, I had experienced more than my fair share of Japanese male-bonding rituals. It was just as well that I'd had some practice, because after our evening's adventures the time had come for us to sleep together – in one of the shared rooms to which travelling companions are assigned in Japanese-style inns, which function as drawing room, bedroom and dining room. Our maid had already laid out the futons for the night, cleared away the dinner and dimmed the two lights with paper shades. I went to the loo, partly to give Masamichi the privacy to get changed... but "went to the loo" is too simple an account of what happened when I confronted the high-tech gizmo bristling with gadgetry that was the toilet. Toilets in Japan derive from two eras, the Stone Age and the Space Age: they are either simple holes in pieces of porcelain, or they are formidable cutting-edge contraptions framed by gleaming control panels and arrays of touch-pad buttons. Some of them look like you can design cars with them, or measure geological movements in the earth's crust.

The only obvious function of this toilet that I could pinpoint with any certainty was that vital bit of kit, the seat heater. But as for that old-fashioned function, the flush, it completely eluded me. After looking everywhere – the control panels, the lid, the seat, the sides, the toilet wall, the light switch – I pressed an incomprehensibly labelled button at random while peering down the bowl. An aluminium robotic arm swung smartly out and fired jets of warm water into my face. Furiously, I hit the button again in order to stop the flow, but without success. Panicking, I pressed every other button I could find in quick succession, and although lots of things happened (the blasts of perfume were a nice touch, as was the tinny rendition of Vaughan Williams's 'Lark Ascending', which I later discovered was more to drown out the acoustics of evacuation than to entertain), the robotic arm continued to jet out warm water. By now the toilet bowl was almost full, so I jammed the lid down, hoping that this would send a clear message to the toilet's central intelligence system – but then the water started seeping out from underneath, together with the traces I'd left of my visit, forming an expanding lake on the floor. Masamichi, mercifully, was in one of his most empathetic modes. Responding to my cries for help, he shouted from outside:

"Press the button next to the button at the left. Emergency button, stops everything."

The murky flood abated.

It was a small step, but I felt I was beginning to master the more elemental aspects of Japanese culture.

7

FREAKY CLEANLINESS

To Westerners it might seem incongruous that the lowly toilet should be taken to such technological heights, or that shopkeepers should spend hours each week fanatically scrubbing floors that are obviously spotless, or that one pair of slippers is required in the living room and another in the bathroom. But Japan's cult of the toilet, and of cleanliness in general, is by no means concerned only with hygiene. Above all it is concerned with appearances – especially of beauty and order. The fact is, under the surface Japan can be absolutely fetid. Some of its hospitals, public offices, and even private houses are among the fithiest, dingiest and untidiest I have ever seen.

You can get a feel for the aesthetic, rather than hygienic, motivation for cleanliness in the writings of the great twentieth-century novelist Tanizaki. His quest for the perfect toilet confronted him with some truly "vexatious problems". Where beauty and hygiene conflict, as they do for Tanizaki with modern, Western-style toilets, he is in no doubt as to which of the two ideals must yield. Rather than having a traditional Japanese toilet, he laments…

...it turns out to be more hygienic and efficient to install modern sanitary facilities – tiles and a flush toilet – though at the price of destroying all affinity with "good taste" and the "beauty of nature"... There is no denying the cleanliness; every nook and corner is pure white. Yet what need is there to remind us so forcefully of the issue of our own bodies... and how very crude and tasteless to expose the toilet to such excessive illumination... In such places the distinction between the clean and the unclean is best left obscure, shrouded in a dusky haze.

At this point Tanizaki's paean to the traditional toilet approaches the realm of the sacred:

The parlour may have its charms, but the Japanese toilet truly is a place of spiritual repose... No words can describe that sensation as one sits in the dim light, basking in the faint glow reflected from the shoji, lost in meditation... And the toilet is the perfect place to listen to the chirping of insects or the song of the birds, to view the moon, or to enjoy any of those poignant moments that mark the change of the seasons. Here, I suspect, is where haiku poets over the ages have come by a great many of their ideas. Indeed one could with some justice claim that of all the elements of Japanese architecture, the toilet is the most aesthetic. (Junichirō Tanizaki, *In Praise of Shadows*, trans. Thomas J. Harper and Edward G. Seidensticker, Vintage, 2001)

This claim that the traditional toilet trumps all the other glories of Japanese architecture – temples, palaces, tea pavilions, shrines – is exorbitant only to the Westernized mind. To Japanese sensibility, or at least to one of its moods, triumph lies not in the monumental, the complete, the illuminated, the brilliant, but in capturing and perfecting the incidental, the partial, the concealed, the shadowy. Though it is pretty eccentric to see the toilet as the finest expression of these latter qualities, it is not, in Japanese terms, wholly absurd.

Not everyone, of course, can aspire to Tanizaki's refinement in these matters. Most Japanese value the ideal of cleanliness less for such exalted aesthetic reasons than for the sake of good order and its associated virtues, such as diligence and dedication. A well-ordered household, like a well-ordered society, must be seen to be spotless – the Confucian equivalent of the Western proverb that "cleanliness is next to godliness". Thus the streets are constantly swept, and no one in their right minds would be seen throwing litter around (though the young, seldom considered to be in their right minds, are increasingly challenging this convention). And thus the redoubtable Japan Toilet Association has been opening the lid on the state of the nation's public conveniences since 1985, maintaining an active network of researchers and designers, running toilet essay competitions, awarding prizes for the best kept toilets in the country, and publishing pamphlets with such catchy titles as *The Restroom Revolution of Japan*.

Flush with its initial success, the JTA has taken its campaign beyond Japan's shores by sponsoring not just an international body called The Privy Council, but also the World Toilet Summit. The inaugural summit was held in Singapore in November 2001, together with an exhibition entitled 'Restroom Asia', just as the rest of the world was focusing on the threat to civilization from global terrorism. Aside from dozens of speeches, the summit's packed agenda

included a mime performance "depicting desirable and un-
desirable toilet behaviour", and guided tours of toilets in
the local zoo.

Like most summits, it agreed to hold another expensive
summit the following year. But unlike most summits
it also managed to set up an entirely new international
bureaucracy – the WTO – an entity with the power to
change the world for the better. It's true that the WTO, or
World Toilet Organization, is yet to exert the same kind
of deep and wide-ranging influence on world affairs as
its rather more controversial WTO namesake, the World
Trade Organization. But it has already shown a defter, more
populist touch than its capitalist counterpart by releasing its
own lyric, 'The World Toilet Song', and proclaiming 19th
November to be World Toilet Day. In a ringing summons to
the peoples of the world, the WTO website declares:

> The purpose of this day is to have people in all
> countries to take action, to increase awareness of
> toilet user's right to a better toilet environment, and
> to demand for it from the toilet owners... On this
> day we would like all toilet users to get involved.
> The public marks the day to practice toilet etiquette,
> the restroom community-at-large celebrates with a
> new declaration for the forthcoming year.

The commitment of this organization to genuine hygiene is
not to be doubted, but in mainstream Japan it's the *appearance*
of cleanliness that really counts. Why else do taxi drivers
and station guards wear gloves, though they seldom touch
anyone, whereas nurses in hospitals often treat desperately
vulnerable and infectious people with bare hands? Why in
this nation of a hundred million raw-fish eaters is there

almost no food contamination, whereas the newspapers abound with reports of patients being needlessly infected, even killed, by unhygienic hospital staff, dialysis machines and blood transfusions? Why do the flawlessly polite clerks at supermarket check-outs dab their index fingers on a little wet towel before packing your groceries, whereas the medic drawing a routine blood sample touches your skin with unwashed and unprotected hands?

The answer is that railway stations, streets, shops and sushi bars are public places, and what goes on in them is witnessed by millions every day. Hospitals, on the other hand, though they are more in need of hygiene than anywhere, are shunted out of the public gaze, where lapses in cleanliness don't offend social order unduly, unless they explode into a scandal. The worst and most secret infectious diseases, such as HIV/AIDS, can be hidden best of all, and are all too often barely recognized as existing. Everybody I consulted agreed that the government systematically conceals the true scale of AIDS, which might be ten or twenty times the official count. As a result, until a few years ago there was minimal health or sex education available for preventing the spread of HIV. Though such unhygienic practices will undoubtedly improve as Japanese society becomes more open, they express one of the darkest sides of the national soul: the habitual lying to preserve appearances; the coldness towards the suffering of those outside one's social group; the haughtiness of the powerful; the indifference, even contempt, for the weak and the misfits; an overwhelming predilection to see dirt swept under the carpet.

8

THE ARCHITECT'S WIFE

A fortnight after visiting the spa at Atami, I met up with
Masamichi's wife, Yuki. Masamichi had gone to a business
event – an all-male affair where endless drinking and exchanges of confidences about girlfriends provided a light-
hearted cover for probing the possibilities of a deal – and
I felt that a good way of thanking him for his hospitality
would be to invite her to dinner.

She was an attractive and energetic woman of about fifty-
five, with an engaging, though nervously random, laugh.
As well as raising two children, she managed the day-to-
day affairs of Masamichi's business – the contracts, invoices
and other administrative chores. Her extraordinarily self-
controlled demeanour betrayed some deep inner confusion,
and this seemed to be centred on how much freedom she
(or any modern Japanese woman) could hope for within a
dull and dutiful marriage. She was obviously preoccupied
by Masamichi's extended absences abroad, his habit of not
returning home until the small hours of the morning, and
his failure to answer his mobile phone when she called.
Though more hurt by his indifference to her than by his
lust for other women, she was by no means resigned to her

49

lot. The question that clearly tantalized her was how far the rules of the game for married women were changing in Japan – and, in particular, whether the greater social acceptability of divorce would give wives more power within their marriages. Change was very much in the air – you felt it everywhere, at least in a great city like Tokyo – but to what extent was it actually happening on the ground?

We met at the station in Kamakura and wandered around trying to decide on a restaurant.

"I really enjoy that you eat me out," she confided.

"Um, yes," I replied; "it's good not to have to cook."

"You know, Japanese men always away work. Or always with other men. No time to eat out wife, even on vacation."

I felt uncertain as to whether her English was faulty or whether she was just pretending to be naive. "Eating out is so much fun," I retorted enthusiastically, "though I think I do it too often" – a reference to my lamentable sloth in the kitchen.

"I like it!" she enthused, "I like it! More eating out is best."

We stopped in front of a small Zen vegetarian restaurant which Yuki remembered from a long time back as being simple but excellent. Judging by its emptiness and air of desolation, it had fallen on hard times. It was a far cry from formal Tokyo restaurants, and going inside it felt like gate-crashing a stranger's home during a family row. Palpable tension was emanating from the open kitchen behind the counter, close to where we sat down. The old master shuffled about, wordlessly directing his younger colleague and a kimono-clad waitress. She was fraught with silent protest – against what I never found out, though I sensed it was against more than her subservience as a waitress or as a woman. All three faces were lined with some insoluble sadness.

Three other customers were sitting at the counter: a seller of goldfish and pet piglets, the owner-chef of a Chinese restaurant, and the toothless proprietor of a nearby soup bar. Their rough but taut faces expressed the immense capacity of the Japanese to endure. The only buoyant character among them was the dealer in goldfish and pet piglets. He explained to everyone how his business was recession-proof: in good times people buy goldfish as an adornment to their good luck, and in bad times as a consolation for their misfortune. The same logic applied to piglets, more or less. The owner of the Chinese restaurant, who was Japanese, was sunk in gloom, bemoaning the conservatism of the locals, who wouldn't eat any Chinese food except for noodle soup; all the convoluted delicacies he had been trained to prepare went for nothing out here in the sticks.

So why did he choose to learn Chinese cooking, I asked him through Yuki, when Japanese food was so good – and appreciated by his clients?

"Chance," he answered. "Just happened to meet an old cook from China who taught me the tricks."

"Never trust the Chinese," the old master put in, with irrelevant spite. Then, in an anxiously enquiring aside to me: "Are you Chinese?"

Yuki assured him that although I was an odd *gaigin*, I was not a hitherto unknown species of round-eyed Chinaman. He looked content at having spared my feelings.

"Things Chinese are occasionally all the rage here," the other man continued, "then we turn our backs on them for a few decades. Ignore China. Ignore the world. This is always happening in Japan."

I felt intensely observed by the three diners. At first, on my arrival, they had studiedly ignored me. Then they had started casting furtive glances in my direction, trying to size up the extent to which my foreignness was admirable or contemptible, and enquiring whether I could really manage the local food. (It's so irritating that, however long you've been among Japanese, they almost always ask if you can use chopsticks, worry whether you will like raw fish – the word sushi being too unapproachably Japanese to risk on the uncomprehending foreigner – and explain that *matcha* is green tea.) Finally, the chef enquired with brutal directness what configuration of random fate could possibly explain my bizarre presence in his country.

Yuki tried to impress them not just by dropping the name of Tokyo University but by pointedly mentioning my title, *Tetsugaku no sensei*, Professor of Philosophy. In smarter restaurants I had found that this title possessed almost magical powers to secure my right to exist, and could even bag a reservation when all tables were said to be fully booked. But the master, who had a habit of punning with a sort of weary dutifulness, as if his clients expected it as part of the service, was decidedly unimpressed by *Tetsugaku no sensei*. "Sounds like *Ketsugaku no sensei*," he quipped – Professor of Arseholes. An arseologist.

Meanwhile the owner of the soup bar – who kept interrupting the master's wisecracks, so as to prevent him from dominating the proceedings – was playing up to his self-appointed role as the local eccentric, confident that his mordant wit could see off all-comers. Unfortunately, no one could really understand what he was saying: all his teeth had been lost in the Second World War, when he had fallen out of a train into a gutter during a send-off party for soldiers going to Manchuria. Since then he had failed to save enough money to buy dentures. In fact no one in this forlorn eatery, barring the waitress, had a full set of teeth – which might have been why they all ordered *chawanmushi*, a delicious and inexpensive savoury egg custard filled with seasonal vegetables, which certainly wasn't doing anything to shore up the owner's profits.

"You ever enjoy older woman?" Yuki asked, after having tried for some time to wean me off the banter with the other customers. Her expression was light-hearted, and it was by no means certain that she was advancing her own candidature.

"My first girlfriend was twelve years my senior. Since then, they've always been my age or younger. Do Japanese men often go for older women?" I asked, trying to deflect her question.

"Very common after forty-five. But only as mistress. And nobody admit it," she added mischievously. "Modern Japanese girl don't understand how treating a man. Forgot real looking after things. Forgot all tradition. I am very sorry. I love men who appreciate real woman attention…"

"Yes…"

"…and also good food."

"Yes…"

"My dream is establish bar in my house, cook for husband on one side, and watch him eat on other side."

"Oh yes!" I muttered, involuntarily.

"Actually, this give me even more pleasure than husband eating me out."

I could see her point.

"When he enjoy his food I am so happy. Food bind man and woman."

These were arguments with which I could wholeheart-edly identify – unity through food; food as love potion; the libidinal power of the palate. I responded enthusiastically to Yuki's fantasy of a counter in the home at which a husband is offered a suite of delicacies by his wife, who would in turn regard this pampering not as service but as bounty, or affirmation, which she alone could confer. I also relished the freedom to enjoy a fantasy about which I would need to be more guarded back home, if not downright ashamed. The scenario seemed perfectly wonderful.

"Don't you think only older woman understand needs of real man?" she said huskily.

"So how about your future?" I countered, trying both to dodge the question and seem as if I were addressing it.

"Me?" Her face crumpled into a deep, oddly charming sadness. "I don't know. What I can do?" She shrugged her shoulders pessimistically. "Nothing to do. We Japanese woman just trapped. Just accept man's behaviour. Last week, for example, I find thirty-two page letter in purple ink from woman client of our company, a widow, not even very attractive, complaining that Masamichi try to seduce her and that he boast her his many girlfriends, even in office. What I should do? So embarrassing for wife. She is important customer, so response necessary. Of course, he too lazy to reply. But how can I reply for him in this case?" Then, after a pause, as if deciding then and there to rebel, she said: "You know, I don't accept such behaviour any more. I used to be good Japanese wife, quiet, never complain. Now I consider divorce. Only freedom for me. My children will support me. But he will refuse. He will give me no money. So how should I live?" She looked at me with red eyes, trying to control herself, then broke down and buried her head in my shoulder.

The others stared unashamedly, trying to figure out what was going on. Their confusion wasn't helped by my inability to stifle a snigger – while Yuki was still sobbing gently on my shoulder – at the thought of the thirty-two page letter in purple ink from a widow shocked to find herself being seduced by her architect, while he was making it clear to her that she was by no means the only one.

"She love you!" the soup-bar owner shouted jauntily out of the toothless aperture of his mouth.

"Woman is woman," declared the master, smiling at me with a sarcastic I've-seen-it-all-before grin. "You are right," he added, "laughter is best response for woman tears."

His subordinates stared sullenly.

"And his mother will support him with everything," Yuki complained miserably. "She always hate me. I don't exist for her. She will be so happy when I am out of his company."

"She hated you all these years?" I asked. "For thirty years?"

"Yes, always. I am not her family, not her blood."

"But surely she values your contribution to the business?" I said, puzzled at her mother-in-law's hostility. From what Masamichi had told me of his mother, it seemed that although she was stubborn, bigoted, and blindly doting on her son, she knew when to be pragmatic. And it was obvious that Masamichi, though a skilful architect and shrewd negotiator, couldn't administrate his way out of a paper bag. Without Yuki's organizational skills the business would have gone bankrupt or been closed by the tax inspectors long ago.

"No, she think I do nothing in Masamichi's business. All these years she only complain, only accuse me that I use my husband."

"Would she accept your children working for the business?" I asked, trying to test the blood theory.

"Of course. They are same genes. But I am alien genes. For her, any wife is alien blood. That's it."

Again she started crying.

There was silence in the restaurant. The waitress had disappeared by now, and the men were looking at us with awkward compassion. Yuki was embarrassed by her tears, but the others were neither embarrassed nor amused any more. On the contrary, they seemed saddened and perplexed.

Later, when we got up to leave, the confused melancholy abruptly gave way to ebullient bonhomie: no nation can manage a sudden transition of mood as genuinely and smoothly as the Japanese. The three customers shook my hand effusively, each holding it in a hoary clasp of affirmation, as though to mark our mutual participation in the magnificent disaster of being alive. I discreetly freed myself. Since in Japan you almost never get touched in public unless you are a dog, and then only if you are tiny and toy-like or else huge and shaggy, I took this unusual gesture of affinity as a striking acceptance of my foreignness and, in its warmth and firmness, as a signal of the irrepressibility of all real contact between people, even when fleeting.

It had been an evening full of humour and sadness and affection and naturalness, and of gently intense connections. Yet, like most Japanese expressiveness, however ardent, it didn't linger long, but seemed to rise up into the night and vanish, like smoke. It was genuine, yet left no residue. I went home; and still I felt alone.

9

Fully Frontal

The young are for the most part brash, confident and relaxed. The difference between them and their parents is starker than in any previous generation gap in Japan, and is increasing all the time. Their manner, dress, tastes and easygoing exterior parallel those of young people around the world. Indeed, far from merely aping foreign fashions, Japanese youth is now busily creating them. The guinea pigs for this new export industry are the legions of teenagers prowling about areas like Shibuya in western Tokyo, with their brightly dyed hair curled or plaited or twisted into punky spikes, and their iPods blaring out the latest J-pop hits. Girls are as different from tripping geishas as you can get, although they frequently trip up on their eight-inch-high platform shoes – a fad marked, not surprisingly, by a spate of broken ankles and dainty limping. Far from the whitened powder face and figure-concealing *kimomo* of the geisha, they are decked out in garish make-up, huge fake nails, stick-on eyelashes, crimson, yellow or green hair extensions, and tiny miniskirts wrapped around their slender hips like loincloths. Perhaps underneath it all they remain as Japanese as their parents, but they certainly seem utterly different, and bemusing, to their elders.

One thing is clear: they love sex. High-school students claim to be too busy or segregated for it, but the evidence on trains and public thoroughfares suggests otherwise. The old taboo of kissing in public has been brazenly cast aside. On off-peak commuter trains, I often saw schoolchildren absorbed in advanced petting, having consumed their fast food and cast the empty cartons onto an adjacent seat. Predictably, the liberties taken by Japanese youth gravely worry their elders, from parents who fear for their children's careers, to government bureaucrats who (somewhat hypocritically) complain of an "ethical vacuum", to captains of industry who wonder how purple-plumed punks will ever be turned into good corporate warriors. Almost everybody seems baffled by what is really going on in these libertine heads. Explanations for the phenomenon of *jiko-chu*, or self-centredness, abound: poor parental guidance, dietary changes, mental dysfunction. I stumbled across one of the more original theories while leafing through *The Daily Yomiuri*, a major national newspaper. Under the headline 'Young People Suffer From Immature Frontal Lobe', a professor of brain science from the distinguished University of Hokkaido was claiming that public displays of *jiko-chu*, such as kissing, changing clothes in public and applying make-up in trains, could be put down to inadequacies in the frontal lobe, the brain's most developed region. In his article, which covered much of the front page of the newspaper's special New Year supplement on the future of Japan, Professor Toshiyuki Sawaguchi insisted that young people behave exactly like patients suffering from disorders of this part of the brain:

> These people ignore the situations or people around them. For instance, they suddenly become

upset in quiet gatherings, making obscene remarks
about women walking along the street, or acting
disgracefully in a crowd.

The really bad news, according to the professor, was that
most human abilities – language learning, self-control,
sympathy with others, determining one's goal in life or
indeed any activity at all for whatever end – turn out to
depend on the frontal lobe, so "there will be no hope for
Japan in the 21st century" unless "immediate measures" are
taken "to remedy the situation". These measures included
attending to the Mongoloid brain's scientific requirements
"to be raised slowly and carefully in large families and be
exposed to complex social relationships". Since "racially,
the Japanese are Mongoloid", such an environment was
essential to ensuring that Japanese children's frontal lobe
develops properly. Sadly, "Westernization" and a declining
birth rate were threatening any return to traditional child-
rearing practices, so the Professor advocated grabbing the
bull by the horns and establishing special schools to help
children develop their frontal lobes – for which a nationwide
initiative embracing government, local communities and
parents was required. And he concluded, in ringing tones:

> Let's establish "schools to nurture the frontal lobe" –
> I offer this proposal to make the 21st century bright
> for Japan.

Judging by their brassiness and, in the case of many of
the undergraduates, their indolence, my students at Tokyo
University had specific frontal-lobe problems of their own.
Their deference was restricted to my first meeting with
them – when I was duly bowed to and addressed as *sensei*

(teacher). Thereafter they were bold, informal and to the point. They came and went from my lectures when they felt like it, nodded off when they were tired or bored, asked direct and usually excellent questions, left their mobile phones on, and giggled, whispered and flirted during classes as students do everywhere. The tone was set at the beginning of the academic year, when they all introduced themselves. Without a hint of shyness, they each stood up to speak. Their interests seemed to coalesce around the grimmer German philosophers. A dapper young man, dressed in an immaculate suit, said he wasn't sure if he liked philosophy at all, but was giving it a try, beginning with Hegel's *Phenomenology of Spirit* (rather like choosing Joyce's *Ulysses* as one's first reading material, instead *The Hungry Hamster*). Another, very self-possessed, said he had started with Kierkegaard's *Sickness unto Death* at sixteen and had just finished Heidegger's *Being and Time* – which he read in the original German, a task from which many, if not most, Germans would shrink. A rather attractive and taciturn girl, who compulsively scratched her arms with her fingernails and then picked at the scabs, and who I was sure would be overcome by shyness when her turn came, stood up and declared her special interests to be euthanasia, Heidegger, and Novalis's *Hymn to the Night* – a pretty unnerving combination even for the strictest devotee of the Teutonic mind.

At dinner afterwards, discussion was more light-hearted. This time, the students were all asked to introduce their hobbies. Again, no one was reserved; many were gregarious to the point of exhibitionism. One young man – the thinnest youth I have ever seen – said his hobby was Sumo wrestling. I was attempting to conjure up this unlikely spectacle when his neighbour said that he enjoyed watching his puppies bite each other. The taciturn girl said that she played Satie and Chopin for a few hours a day, some of the time as entertainment at weddings. And funerals. Another, the son of a farmer, who modestly claimed that he had been "born a philosopher", enjoyed visiting fish markets with his parents, but had given this up in order to learn German, French and English, so as to read "all philosophy texts in the original". Someone else, wearing a T-shirt which mysteriously declared "HELL AWAITS", said that he really wanted to fall in love with some subject now – if not philosophy then another – because "after twenty-five falling in love becomes much harder".

I sat there wondering why Japan is normally considered to be so inscrutable. Was I missing something? How was it that my discussions with people had been so fluid, whether with young or old, conformists or mavericks? Perhaps my own frontal lobe was being rigorously challenged? Or was my apparently easy integration part of the trick that Japan plays on novices – gently drawing them in before, as it were, spitting them out, brutally and unexpectedly?...

10

COVER-UPS AND CONSPIRACIES

It was a very hot summer, and even the most stoical Japanese were complaining. Their faces looked swollen and immobile, as if they were trying to hold their breath until autumn. All summer they maintained that countenance, fixed like a Noh mask, even inside air-conditioned offices and subways. In the evenings typhoons would sometimes swoop in, battering the houses and soaking the land, until the next morning when the blazing sun would evaporate the rainwaters back into the already humid air. It was a Sisyphian task for Japan Inc. to keep functioning in these conditions, and for its ranks of corporate warriors to sustain their prowess on the commercial battlefield when they were so visibly burdened by the fight against thirty-six degrees centigrade and 90% humidity. In these sweltering conditions, every piece of bad news took on a particularly ominous tone. Underneath the disciplined veneer of public life, a sense of doom was taking hold.

There was dark talk about accidents in the nuclear power industry which had been hidden for years, and about the absence of even the most basic safety procedures. There were the pharmaceutical companies accused of marketing products that hadn't been properly tested or were of dubious efficacy – government licences to sell the drugs had been obtained by bribing Ministry of Health officials, it was said. There were the corrupt savings funds. All this, people said, was just the tip of the iceberg of Japan's culture of lying; it was the result of a society valuing collective harmony so obsessively that almost any action, however unethical, is tolerated in order to preserve order.

You could really feel ordinary people's anger about the continuing secretiveness, conservatism and corruption of so much big business and bureaucracy. Yuki's attitude was typical. Once, when I stopped to buy some Vitamin C tablets, she treated me as though I were mad.

"Probably just contain white powder," she said. "No vitamins there at all! If customer can't find out, manufacturer will cheat."

I asked her whether a government health agency, analogous to the Food and Drug Administration in the US, didn't monitor the sale of drugs.

"No way," she laughed. "There is drugs agency, yes, but they have too few staff. Staff take bribes from the pharmaceutical companies to clear products."

Another time, when I was talking about a local government programme that offered free medical screening to citizens, praising it as an excellent example of preventive medicine, she looked at me as if I were not merely an unsuspecting *gaigin*, but criminally naive about Japanese ways:

"Mayors only offer these tests because big medical companies bribe them to buy expensive equipment like X-ray machine," she lectured me. "Have to do something with millions of dollars of useless machinery."

I suspected Yuki's cynicism was exaggerated until my encounter, not long afterwards, with a highly articulate doctor, trained in the United States, whom I met at a concert in Tokyo. He had just had a minor operation for a kidney stone – not at his own hospital, a major Tokyo public health centre, but at an exclusive private clinic. I asked him why he refused to be a patient in his own hospital.

"The surgeons regularly make small mistakes," he said, "like taking the wrong organ out."

"The wrong organ?"

"Sometimes out of the wrong patient," he added, as an afterthought.

"But surely you, as an insider, can insist on having one of the best surgeons?"

"No, once you are under anaesthetic, anyone can operate. You'll never know who did it. Nobody will tell the truth. And many of them don't care about you."

"Many of them?" Surely that wildly overstated the point.

"They stop caring after a few years on the job. The older surgeons behave like gods. They give the younger ones all the uninteresting operations, no power, and so much work that they easily make mistakes. They keep the interesting stuff for themselves. But that is dangerous too, because they experiment on patients in order to obtain scientific information and advance their careers."

"Experiment? You mean innovate?"

"No, experiment, even if it endangers the patient's life. This happens in many big hospitals."

"What happens if something goes wrong?"

"They lie about the reason. Nobody can find out the truth. If they accidentally kill the patient, they falsify the death certificate. They just say the patient died of pneumonia or some other complication."

"Can't the relatives ask for a second opinion?"

"Yes, sometimes, but doctors close ranks, so relatives can't discover truth. Here in Japan, nothing is a crime unless it's discovered. No accountability."

"Accountability would help things along," I agreed.

"Actually accountability can be a big problem too," he said. "You see, of course, most doctors try to avoid accidental death, so in some difficult cases they recommend not operating at all. They prefer to give the wrong diagnosis than to accept responsibility for failure of treatment. I have known many people being given a false diagnosis by senior doctors if they think treatment will be risky. No one ever finds out."

This business about deliberate misdiagnosis was as shocking as the experimentation. Incompetence was one thing, but purposeful error of this kind was almost beyond belief. Perhaps it occurred infrequently. Perhaps he was exaggerating. But I began to understand why public mistrust of large organizations – and especially of the "iron triangle" of big business, bureaucracy and politics – was so widespread.

Masamichi agreed that ethical standards were deplorably low. He too spoke of patients being "experimented" on by ambitious doctors in large urban hospitals. And he had his own horror stories to tell: of a woman who had died in a small, private clinic shortly after childbirth, while the only nurse on duty was out at lunch and the doctor was on the golf course; and of another friend who had been mistakenly advised to abort her pregnancy on medical grounds, but who, thankfully, refused the advice and now had a healthy child of three. But Masamichi didn't concede that there were fundamental flaws in the system itself, such as the huge difficulty of whistle-blowing in a national culture of secrecy and group loyalty. Instead, he thought that people such as the doctors I had heard about were becoming apathetic and unscrupulous because Japan had lost confidence in itself. According to Masamichi, the nation's self-esteem had been severely eroded by discrimination against Japanese exports by the United States and Europe, a persistently high Yen engineered by devious foreigners, and the wholesale Americanization of Japan, which had alienated it from its "true self" and made it "sick with confusion". Quickly expanding his argument, he was soon telling me that these ills in turn resulted from the machinations of an international Jewish conspiracy headed by successive bosses of the US Federal Reserve System. Over the years of Japanese decline, from about 1991 onwards, the Fed had been run by Alan Greenspan, while the US Treasury had been controlled by Jews like Robert Rubin and Larry Summers. Wall Street was in the grip of Semitic cohorts, and Europe, with its Rothschilds and Lazards, followed suit. Bill Gates was a Jew intent on world domination. The aim was to destroy Japan before buying it, and eventually the rest of the world, on the cheap.

"You mean like the 'Hollywood conspiracy' of the 1930's?" I interjected, expecting that my reference to Japan's fascist period would provoke him to instant silence.

Masamichi looked at me blankly.

"The plot to assassinate Charlie Chaplin when he visited Japan," I reminded him.

"Oh yes, you mean right-wing sympathizers who bring dictatorship to power in the 1930s," he said with a broad smile. "They think Chaplin making Communist propaganda in Japan. How stupid they were! Chaplin just a comic. But Jewish conspiracy not comic!"

This view wasn't a million miles from the thinking that nearly dispatched the great man to an early grave. His would-be assassins had reckoned that doing away with

him would provoke his Jewish sponsors in Hollywood to
demand war with Japan, a war which America would surely
lose and which would therefore rid Japan of the evils of
Western democratic capitalism. So Chaplin's murder would
protect Japan from both communism and capitalism, and, in
killing these two birds with one stone, leave it free to pursue
its authentic national path free of alien creeds.

No wonder people inspired by this sort of logic got
their country into such trouble.

Now the really odd thing about Masamichi's quirky
theory was that its tone wasn't bitter, let alone murderous.
But then racism in Japan seldom is. In many Western
countries, most obviously Germany in the 1930s, racism
has been fuelled by deep hatred and, to that extent, remains
a *relationship* – indeed, in its own disgusting way, a passionate
one. To vent one's furious loathing on innocent scapegoats
is to be fixated on them; to murder them is to acknowledge
their existence. But in Japan, there tends to be *complete*
dissociation from the excluded "Other".

This is why victims of racial stereotyping can even
attract mild admiration there. Masamichi's theory of the
worldwide Jewish conspiracy contained just such a note
of wistful admiration, because at least the Jews, unlike the
Japanese, were still capable of organizing something properly,
and doing so to their own clear advantage. Indeed, the Jews,
in his stylized image, exhibited all the characteristics that
the Japanese respect and like to claim for themselves: ethnic
homogeneity, absolute group solidarity, ruthless clarity of
purpose, high intelligence, excellent education, stubborn
courage, a sense of their own "uniqueness", and a refusal to
settle for second best. Part of Japan's problem, as Masamichi
saw it, was that as these qualities were being lost, the country
was becoming vulnerable to manipulation. As to the more

obvious reasons behind Japan's problems – such as reckless speculation in the 1980s, lack of financial transparency, rampant bureaucracy, the stifling of innovation, corruption – Masamichi, unlike Yuki, was silent about them. He was much more open than many Westerners would be about his marriage, his mistresses, his finances, his children; but like most of the men I met, when it came to Japan and its real weaknesses he was persistently evasive and silent. As a friend and a foreigner, I had the right to delve into his family but not into his country.

However deep the iceberg of Japan's moral malaise might be – and it is probably very deep indeed – there is little pressure to reform the culture of cover-ups and conspiracies, except when a massive crisis is in the offing, as when huge Japanese banks teetering on the brink of insolvency were threatening to bring down the whole economy. What kind of crisis is needed to ensure that hospitals will take better care of their patients, or that airlines will really act on major safety lapses, or that nuclear power plants will not falsify their safety records, is impossible to tell.

11

Seitai and the Hypochondriac

"Don't worry, be snappy!" Yuki bantered, as she picked me up from Tokyo University one brilliant afternoon, the air clear and mellow, and the sky a canopy of navy blue. "Please decide decisively," she continued, as I got into her car with some hesitation, wondering what I was letting myself in for.

For weeks I had prevaricated about going to see her *Seitai* healer, who practised in Kawasaki, on the outskirts of Tokyo. It was not that I was frightened, as such: he sounded harmless enough, something like an exotic form of masseur who specialized in gently pressing the acupuncture points. Nor was I concerned about having no ailments to present to him: as a certified hypochondriac, I have always regarded symptoms as optional extras when visiting a doctor. Nor did I suspect him of being unprofessional: Yuki was a very down-to-earth woman, and I trusted her to avoid quacks. What worried me, I think for the first time ever in Japan, was just being a foreigner – whether I could handle him and whether he could handle me.

As we approached Kawasaki, the huge red sun was setting over tangles of pylons and double-decker expressways, and the evening sky was criss-crossed by darkish streaks of pollution. A few lefts and rights further on and we were in deep suburbia, with its tiny box-like houses, neat little gardens, and narrow lanes which double up as children's playgrounds. The house was at the end of a cul-de-sac. As we entered the second floor practice, I felt my worst fears confirmed; it was packed with onlookers who were waiting their turn for treatment, watching the master at work with a reverence that made me distinctly uneasy. Surely they would all crack up laughing to see a *gaigin* insert his cumbersome alien body into this rarified atmosphere, like a car wreck dumped in a summer meadow.

"You change," Yuki advised me in a whisper.

"Change? Into what?"

"Into socks."

"Socks?"

Did I have to be naked except for socks? The idea of lying down in a room full of ogling Japanese, exposing my hairy chest and legs while all the men and women checked out what lay between, whether admiringly or disparagingly, was not a soothing one. I knew that the Japanese were disdainful about even slight coverings of fat, and I had been so gluttonous with sushi as to be perhaps the first person ever to gain weight on the stuff. I was aware of being a very poor ambassador for the Western male torso.

"Here," she said. "Take the socks, and this head scarf."

She handed the socks to me, one by one – impossibly small socks suited to her impossibly small feet. Mickey Mouse was leaping playfully around the ankles. I eyed them reluctantly. But what choice did I have? I feared the pair on my feet smelt like a cheese factory after the long morning walk from Tokyo Station to the university, and after a hot half-day of striving to interest indifferent students in

Kant's concept of autonomy. Such odours might well have interfered with the master's healing art.

"That's it? Just Mickey Mouse socks, and a head scarf?" I asked her gulping, as I started taking off my trousers.

"No, no," she replied, with a giggle. "Keep on shirt and trousers. But remove all metal objects, like belt and watch. They disturb treatment. By the way, this scarf not for wearing. Please put it under your head when you lying down to protect mat from dirty hair. And dribble," she added.

Fair enough.

We got changed silently – she into special baggy trousers and a T-shirt, me into her spare socks – then crept into a long rectangular room containing ninety-six *tatami* mats and about two dozen silent acolytes. The master was hovering squat over a patient lying on her front, his eyes closed in fervent concentration, his hands touching her lower back on either side. Every so often he let out a long, deep grunt.

I liked his profile. It was sensitive and extraordinarily gentle, suggesting a pure receptivity unimpeded by haste or vanity or suspicion.

Apart from odd sighs and shuffles from patients preparing themselves for treatment, the silence was broken only by a clutch of children who were sniggering at the *gaigin* in their midst, and by a couple exchanging whispered confidences. A woman kneeling in a corner occasionally let out a mighty growl, threw her head down between her folded legs and flailed her arms around the sides of her ribcage as if in a trance, though no one seemed to take any notice of this strange warm-up exercise.

Then in a soft, infinitely courteous, voice:

"*Dozo!*" (Please.)

Yuki tapped me on the shoulder and gestured towards the master, who had just beckoned one of us over. Don't I have to wait my turn? I wondered. To jump the queue, whether out of the master's politeness to a foreigner or, worse still, out of a misunderstanding on my part, would compound my embarrassment.

"Us?" I mouthed at the master, "me?" and I gestured vaguely at myself and Yuki.

"*Dozo*," the master repeated, looking at me with his intimidating combination of gentleness and intensity.

I ventured to get up, but couldn't quite manage it; I had been sitting on folded knees for a long time, in order not to look too alien, and my legs had gone to sleep. Again I tried to stand up, using both hands to push myself to my feet – the ultimate in uncool: the proper Japanese way is to go from kneeling to standing without propping yourself up. But my legs were only half-alive, and with a bang I fell backwards onto my behind. A couple of people tittered. I flushed scarlet, then tried to slide across to the master by pushing backwards with my hands. When I finally made it, with all the motor skills of an eighteen-month-old toddler, he was expressing dissatisfaction with me in his gentle un-hurried way.

This turned out to have nothing to do with the comedy act I had just unleashed on him. He had wanted me to sign in. And to pay the fee in advance. Crumbs, it was 30,000 Yen: nearly $300! This seemed steep for fifteen minutes of treatment for no discernible symptoms. But I was too flustered to care, desperately longing to get these booby-trapped preliminaries behind me and lie down so that I couldn't see all those bemused eyes staring at me.

I duly signed in, my signature the only Western script in a sea of kanji. Then I realized I didn't have enough money on me; as so often in Japan, they didn't take credit cards. At this point, I felt I was losing the plot. It was senseless getting treatment, even for my non-existent ailments, if I was this tense. I asked Yuki to go first, despite the master's courtesy in offering me that privilege, so that I could try to wind down, and if possible learn from her example how to be a patient patient.

It seemed to be pretty straightforward: you knelt before the master, bowed to each other simultaneously – the patient, of course, offering the lower bow – and then lay down on a long, narrow cotton strip, which ran down the middle of a larger mat, placing your clean scarf under your head. But it was important not to touch the master's mat before the formal greeting. This inaugurated the session and permitted you to cross the threshold from public to private – a key transition in Japan, which demands rituals of respect, whether the threshold is visible, as in the *genkan* of every Japanese home, where you remove your shoes and replace them with slippers, or invisible, as in the progressive grades of familiarity between colleagues.

It was hard to see exactly what he was doing to Yuki. He appeared to be touching or pressing her at special points down her back and legs, while he knelt at her side. Then he straddled her and, eyes closed, pressed smartly down on each side of the base of her spine. Occasionally, he cupped his hands above a particular spot and let out a deep groan that tapered off into a long sigh. He followed more or less the same procedure when she turned over onto her back, before discharging her with a couple of gentle pats on her shoulder. She got onto her knees again, slid backwards beyond the border of his mat, bowed deeply to him, and then stretched herself out in a corner to rest.

He beckoned me with a nod that was entirely untainted

by my earlier false start. A greeting as fresh as the first one. Respectful, professional, proportional. I lay on my tummy, trying to trust his hands, and could feel the extraordinary heat of his fingertips through my shirt as they touched me. He wasn't doing much at this stage. I think he was listening through his fingers, attuning all his senses. This was receptivity without preconceptions, tender and involved. Under those burning fingers, my anxiety was evaporating.

"Please turn over."

I flipped onto my back, taking in a roomful of curious eyes and able now to see his own – which from underneath looked feverishly focused, almost fanatical, despite their deep gentleness. He knelt by my right side and repeated his careful probe, mainly around my abdomen and pelvis. I felt nothing remarkable except for the heat again. His palms were like a baby's: soft, clean and barely wrinkled, though he couldn't have been a year under forty-five. As he touched me, he would raise his head slightly, his chin jutting up into the air, like a blind man concentrating on his steps. When he finished a series of probes, he would lower it again and sigh affirmatively, as if he had just heard a perfectly rounded musical phrase brought to completion.

He was going back over my abdomen from left to right, and I was starting to relax, when I suddenly winced at a stabbing pain on my right side, a couple of inches below the ribcage. Nothing Yuki had said prepared me for this, and nothing he had done could explain it: his touch had been exceedingly light and cautious.

"I just moved your liver," he admitted.

"Moved my liver?" Where? How? Why?

He smiled mysteriously, but at this point an enigmatic response was definitely not what I was looking for. I wanted full and unambiguous reassurance that he hadn't harmed me.

"Your liver has blockages," he said, as if this explained everything. "I moved your inner energy and it hit the blockages. That's why you're in pain."

The spectre of fatal damage to my liver at once appeared before me.

"Do you know *Ki*?" he asked.

"No," I groaned suspiciously, "who's he?"

"*Ki* is nobody. *Ki* is everywhere. Cosmic energy. In our bodies. In the universe."

Oh my God, here we go, I thought to myself, feeling stupid for being hoodwinked by what the West calls "new age" medicine – which in the Confucian countries is as old as the hills. I'd just put my trust in the man's scalding fingertips and he'd gone and ruined my perfectly serviceable liver.

"For health, *Ki* must be balanced and circulate freely in the body," he continued. "When it gets unbalanced, or its circulation is blocked, illness can result, including cancer."

Cancer?

"*Seitai* treatment just makes your own energy flow, so that no part of your body can become lazy or blocked."

If this had been a philosophy seminar, I'd have enjoyed debating this *Ki*. After all, it has lots of precedents, in the West as well as in the East: Plato's *eros*, Schopenhauer's *will*, maybe Einstein's energy/mass relationship, ideas about the "World Soul". I'd probably have dismissed the idea that *Ki* could get blocked in the body as a pretty metaphor, or a non-explanation, or quackery. But this man had produced a splitting pain in my abdomen for which I had no explanation. And *cancer*, I was still reciting to myself...

Anxious and helpless, I felt like a prisoner on a gurney rather than a patient on a mat, and his concern seemed dangerous rather than kind. As for my liver, it hurt like hell.

I couldn't wait for him to sort it out, or at least restore it to its former misery before I incurred the $300 fee.

"Thank you," he said. "Treatment is over."

Over? – when there was a Hoover dam of *Ki* clogging up my internal workings? I rolled over onto my side sullenly, got back on my knees, remembered to bow, resisted punching him, and tried to force myself to relax in a corner. Lying among the other patients while imagining joyous waves of *Ki* flowing unhindered through my body, I consoled myself with the fact that at least I'd been wearing a fresh pair of socks as my vital organs were being monkeyed around with.

"Perhaps the liver trouble was latent, and now it's out in the open, and can be treated," I tried to tell myself, before dismissing this as so much wishful thinking. "Perhaps he *triggered* rather than *produced* the pain," I tried again, dwelling on the world of difference between these two verbs. But it made no difference – my liver was in obvious trouble. I found myself speculating whether Japanese and Western livers were completely different, and that what healed the one could only harm the other, a thought which plunged me back into helpless anxiety.

I left an IOU for 30,000 Yen, repatriated Mickey Mouse, and drove to Ginza with Yuki. For once I blessed the grid-locked traffic, which gave me an opportunity to quiz her on *Seitai* and extract the reassurance I was craving.

"Pain? Liver pain? Pain in the liver?" She sounded absolutely amazed. "I've never ever heard of that," she said to my consternation, shaking her head sadly, as if this were a very unfortunate one-off. "Normally, I only feel better after *Seitai* treatment, all pain and tension goes, and I'm wonderfully relaxed. All my friends say the same. Must be something wrong with you."

I'd been hoping to hear that a short bout of liver pain was an exceptionally promising signal of enduring good health. Yuki's response made me feel like giving up on my existence there and then, as an enterprise beyond hope

The Master's magic had a surprise in store for me, however. Over the next half an hour, I slowly and irresistably sank into relaxation so deep that I lost all interest in worrying, even in talking. And for the first time ever, I was indifferent to eating – food felt invasive, unclean, crude. I was disgusted at the thought of all those bits of vegetable and batter and dead flesh and carcinogenic pickle, snaking their uncouth way through a mile of my gut. I only wanted sleep. The liver pain notwithstanding, my entire being craved rest and privacy and hygiene. I had Yuki cancel a dinner reservation at one of my favourite tempura restaurants, and I went home to bed.

That night I slept eleven hours. I sweated so much that in the morning my pyjamas were drenched, especially on my back and left shoulder.

"Left shoulder," I mused. "That must be significant: after all, I'm a left-hander. Must be loads of *Ki* swimming about on that side... The sweat is probably a healthy discharge of dammed-up *Ki*."

The next day, I contacted the wife of a colleague for advice. I'd only met Keiko a couple of times, but at the bottom of her emails she described herself as *Spiritual Healer, A Divine Healer certified by Clearsight, the State of California and Reiki Healer*. I would normally run a thousand miles from anyone who called themselves a "Divine Healer", but the situation was much too serious for hard-nosed realism – and words like "spiritual", "healer" and, especially, "Clearsight" raised my hopes that Keiko could shed light on the strange world of *Seitai*. I hoped she was up to the job,

and I waited in a state of escalating anticipation and anxiety
for her reply to my email.

> *Dear Simon,*
>
> *We are both so sorry about your pain. It seems really odd. I asked your higher self this morning and it said the pain was a kind of overreaction caused by the man of Seitai, and it also came from your stress. This information came very vaguely, because it is not normal to feel such pain after treatment. I think his energy is so strong and may be left in clients' bodies, which is not good thing. He should not force his energy in your body or aura. But tomorrow I'll check again with your higher self and let you know.*
>
> *Now I can see your liver in red and pink. The Seitai practicioner's energy might have been removed. I did a distant healing for you, and if you still feel uncomfortable now, please let me know. I'll do it again. When I did the healing, I found that you have some stress, anger and disappointment in your liver. Liver tends to gather minor emotions. Anyway, my psychic surgeon says, "Two more days he needs to bare. If he eat suitable food, it will be over this time." Do you trust him or not???*
>
> *Today will be hot. Please take care.*
>
> *Do some deep breezing.*
>
> > *With lots+lots of love, Keiko*

Keiko's explanation merely compounded my sense of
doom, and her remote intervention did not seem to have
any effect. As for her consultation with my higher self,
which by now was probably as disorientated as the rest of
me, she was on a hiding to nothing there. I felt awful. I felt
like a balloon had been inflated in my abdomen. I felt like a
goose that has been force-fed for *foie gras*.

The following week, Yuki assumed I would join her for *Seitai* again. I vacillated. Should I let the master resolve the problem he had created, or should I avoid him at all costs in case he wrecked my kidneys too? In the end I firmly decided I wouldn't go near the old fraud again – not even if he gave me my 30,000 Yen back, not even if he begged me in his irritatingly tranquil way.

Two hours later I was describing my concerns to him in graphic detail, cutting out all circuitous speech and other Japanese niceties. I told him, too, that a divine healer with a Californian diploma had been exceedingly worried about me, and played my trump card – she was a certified *Japanese* divine healer.

He seemed unfazed.

"Yes, your pain should not have lasted so long. Normally, in cases like yours, it disappears after a few hours."

I was terrified he'd be talking about cancer again in no time, but I lay on my tummy while he repeated his meticulous diagnostic procedures.

"You must be especially responsive," he murmured, after asking me to turn over. "Pain is the sign of a responsive body. You have a healing pain, rather than a destructive pain."

Oh, what joy! I had a responsive body? A healing pain? So my pain was virtuous, the reaction of a supremely alert body! I was the proud possessor of a meticulously acute sensory apparatus! My liver had won a reprieve. A huge surge of relief smothered my anxiety. For a few sweet seconds the elation lingered, before I took to wondering whether this might be so much blarney to justify his exorbitant fees or to hide an error behind a compliment… the error that he might have created my unhealthy build-up of *Ki*, my inflated *foie gras* liver, by his own misguided hand.

"How long will the pain last?" I asked him, trying not to sound too desperate in case he lied in order to console me. "It will go in time," was all he promised.

It was not much of a straw to clutch at until my next appointment, but I clutched at it nevertheless. As I left, I put 30,000 Yen into the payment box – at least *this* time, I congratulated myself, I wasn't going to look like a foreign idiot.

The master burst into laughter, and a room full of Japanese with perfectly free-flowing *Ki* followed suit.

"30,000 Yen is membership fee," an assistant explained to me. "Afterwards, session is only 3,000 Yen."

Yuki later told me that this was a *kyokai*, or "circle". Without realizing it, I had become a fully paid-up disciple of a Japanese sect. One, moreover, that seemed to meddle with cosmic energy.

By my next visit, the pain had definitely eased. It was dull, rather than piercing, though exacerbated by exercise and even by breathing deeply. But the master wasn't interested in my carefully noted symptoms, and ignored all my entreaties to explain them. Today he was aiming higher than my liver. After the usual few minutes of having me lie on my front, he asked me to kneel on my heels, Japanese-style. Crouching behind me, he ran his fingers up and down my spine and cupped my head in his hands.

Among the ranks of stiff Westerners, I belong to the very stiffest, those who find more than a minute in this kneeling position excruciatingly painful. The tension of enduring it must have been sending my *Ki* haywire, and the Master duly found a new bottleneck: this time at the back of my head, just behind the crown. As with my liver, pain erupted precisely where his hands had lingered. I felt that same unpleasant pressure, that same unnatural ballooning, which I had come to call the "*foie gras* effect".

In the subsequent, detailed email correspondence with Keiko, she said that this point on the head was the entry point for cosmic energy. The pain showed that I must be especially open to the world spirit – though, she added, it could also mean that I was simply overstrained. "Pain here suggest you are thinking and worrying too much," she warned me. No wonder, I thought; all this *Seitai* treatment was taking its toll. The more *Seitai* I had, the more I needed. I spent another week sleeping the sleep of the dead and dousing my pyjamas in sweat.

In the end I stopped attending *Seitai,* and over time my pains reduced and went away. Memories of the pains I'd had receded, and I thought about the Master with his fiery fingertips less and less, and then not at all, until I returned to London later that summer, when ultrasound tests revealed that I had a spastic colon – a stress-induced condition that can be triggered by, say, scary therapists or unexplained "liver" pains. And my acupuncturist told me that in Chinese medicine "liver" refers not simply to the organ but to a region embracing, yes, the colon, which happened to pass right through the area of my abdominal pain. So the *Seitai* master had been right: the liver and head pains did eventually go. But nobody could explain how his burning hands induced them in the first place.

12

THE WANDERING KNEE

It was a beautiful Friday evening and I was meeting Masamichi and Yuki for dinner. On the train ride into Tokyo, I had the sudden good fortune to glimpse a perfect sunset over Mount Fuji, which occasionally popped into view between cracks in the sixty-kilometre urban mass that stretches between Kamakura and central Tokyo. In the six months since I'd arrived in Japan, I'd never managed to catch sight of it. But there it now was, reclining in stately, symmetrical repose, draped in its famous snowy mantle. A bunch of skyscrapers in front of the Matterhorn or Mont Blanc would seem like a screaming insult to nature, but for some reason the silent elegance of the mountain, and the noisy ugliness of the urban landscape obscuring it most of the time, don't jar with each other. Fuji presides over the absurdly hectic and inelegant city at its feet with no hint of reproach, a living volcano inhabited by the most refined and sovereign of gods.

But my enjoyment of Fuji, and my anticipation of a good dinner, were soon interrupted by acute unease. A man standing next to me in the packed train was rubbing his knee between the legs of a girl seated in front of him.

85

She was in her late teens or early twenties. Neither was looking at the other and both seemed impassive. I looked around at the passengers pressed against me, searching for a lead on what to do. Something? Nothing? Was this one of those assignations that Japanese students sometimes make with older men, in return for expensive clothes and other status symbols to which they otherwise wouldn't have access? Then it became clearer to me that the girl wasn't happy at all: though her expression was taut, her eyes were darting glances at an older lady sitting opposite, her travelling companion, possibly her mother. But the girl didn't move, the older lady didn't help her, and no one else said anything to the man. Confrontation, or even a hint of it, was unthinkable.

For three more stops – a good fifteen minutes – that knee would press and push between the girl's legs. Becoming convinced that she was being fondled against her will, I decided to show the man that I had noticed what he was doing. I stared at him in an invasive, exaggerated fashion, then down at his knee and the girl, and then back up at him. He pretended not to have seen me. I repeated the procedure more aggressively. No one took any notice, not the other passengers, not the man, and not the girl. Clearly an even stronger action was required, something emphatic that would solve the problem immediately. So in order to shame the man publicly, I took the risk of bending down and asking the girl if she was OK. After a brief, blank look at me, she stared straight ahead again without flinching, her face freezing into a deeper expression of simulated unconcern. I got the distinct sense that being spoken to by me was far more distressing for her than being rubbed up by my neighbour. The older lady affected not to notice what I'd done. The knee continued its forays between the legs.

What was going on? I was starting to feel that *I* was doing something unsavoury, not the chubby pervert next to me. After weighing up my options, I decided not to give up. I was going to up the ante and declare restrained war on this man's behaviour. I tapped him on the shoulder brusquely and very publicly, I pointed at his leg as though it were a turd on a cheese counter, I sarcastically imitated his knee movements with my index finger, I tried to stare him out, and I crossed my forearms – an emphatic and ubiquitous Japanese gesture meaning "please stop". That would do it...

He glanced at me vacantly, lazily rubbed at the corner of his eye as if trying to see me better, gently cleared his throat – and got to work with his knee again. So the knee went in and out, the girl stared glassily ahead, the older lady looked on blankly, and the other passengers still affected not to have noticed what the man was doing nor how I was responding. Nothing, short of physically grabbing hold of him and hauling him to another part of the carriage, could influence the course of events. I was still thinking about what to do next as the train pulled into a station. When it came to a stop – and not a moment before – the girl and the older lady stood up, politely squeezed past the assailant, and got off. The back of the girl's T-shirt said KOOL DOG: EASY TAKE. As the doors shut and they walked away together, I saw them begin talking animatedly. I watched them until the escalator glided them out of my sight.

For all I know, the girl was saying "Did you *see* what that foreigner did to me?"

13

SHINJUKU BLUES

Yuki and Masamichi were waiting for me at the south exit of Shinjuku station, supposedly the world's largest, and a place where a rendezvous unaided by a mobile phone is decidedly risky. Still somewhat dislocated by my experience on the train, I felt overwhelmed by all the people spilling into every available space on the vast concourse and the surrounding streets. I followed Masamichi quietly as we stumbled in single file through the dense mass; the crowd, like Tokyo itself, was borderless. When we finally reached the street outside, I felt no less hemmed in than on the packed platforms. Even the night sky, crammed between the buildings and enormous advertising screens, afforded no sense of space, and the further we got from the station, the more urgently I was sucked into that vortex of humanity, noise, activity and desire. Though the crowds were calm and polite – I saw punks regularly making way for the elderly – their concentration was asphyxiating.

Soon we reached a square dominated on one side by a vast video screen that manically blinked with ever-changing images of pop stars, baseball players, fashion models, consumer gizmos and sci-fi clips. This huge, frenzied eye was the unofficial centre of Shinjuku. By comparison with its cascade of moving images, the pullulating crowds upon which it stared down seemed almost motionless, as if mesmerized by this great Cyclops. People of all ages milled about, meeting, waiting, posing, coming, going. Clusters of drunken businessmen in identikit suits benignly groped their way towards the station and the long commute home. Cacophonies of giggles and J-pop tunes emanated from groups of girls perching precariously on their platform shoes, girls ogled and baited by youths in tight trousers, open shirts and mandatory poses of laughter and ease. These ogling boys seemed enviably at peace with the world, delightfully free of the awkwardness and festering resentment of so many of their Western peers.

A Buddhist monk in orange-brown robes stood stock still in the flowing streams of people, his unflinching eyes just visible beneath his straw hat, his posture so taut with self-possession that he made begging seem the most dignified, difficult and profound of occupations. Here and there shifty-looking men in long coats or tuxedos handed out leaflets advertising sexual services of various orientations. Everywhere people were on the move – swarms of them on the great thoroughfares, in small alleys, filling and pouring out of the subways, in perpetual circulation, with just a few hours' respite for sleep before migrating all over again. And, fleetingly visible between thousands of hurrying feet, I glimpsed the first homeless people I had seen in Japan, resting on the cardboard boxes which would be their beds for the night...

Shinjuku – a vast, strange, unchoreographed street dance.

We moved on towards the west of Shinjuku, where Masamichi had reserved a dinner table on the top floor of a gleaming glass tower. Girls in immaculate red uniforms beckoned us into a cavernous lift and bowed deeply as the doors silently closed. A few moments later, the Tokyo that had been subsuming me – the mass of people hurrying, harrying, groping, soliciting, imprecating, commuting, begging, milling – lay spread out beneath us, horizonless and motionless, both unbearably homogeneous and unfathomably intricate, a vista at once enervating and consoling.

We ordered *shabu-shabu* – paper-thin slices of "superprime" Kobe beef, which we were to cook at the table in a boiling broth – and fresh vegetables such as shiitake mushrooms, chrysanthemum leaves and Chinese cabbage. The beef wasn't any old super-prime. Its succulently sensuous texture and its sweet, buttery taste requires an aristocratic strain of cattle, imported centuries ago from the great plains of Manchuria, which are plied with grass soaked in beer and with grain laced with sake, and which enjoy not just regular massage but even the occasional course of acupuncture. One of the reasons for all this bovine luxury is to relax the animal and so achieve a more mellifluous, less stringy and savage-tasting meat than your average stressedout heifer could yield. Other aims of the pampering are more subtle: the beer and sake encourage the right microbes to grow in the cow's stomach for extracting unusually refined flavours from the grass, while the massage and acupuncture help to disperse the fat in the muscles and give the meat its gracefully marbled patterns of red, pink and white.

As with all Japanese cooking, unsurpassed ingredients are only the beginning. Timing is the next challenge. A minute more or less in the broth makes the difference between nuanced succulence and tough tastelessness. We were shown the basics by a lovely waitress in a spotless pink apron who quietly prepared me a morsel cooked just enough to achieve a delicious array of flavours and a tender, juicy texture. It seemed a straightforward matter of counting the time. But, as ever, it wasn't easy to master. Whether you held the beef still or moved it in the broth had a crucial effect. And the size of each slice, its fat content, and the effect on the temperature of the broth of cooking other foods with the beef, all had to be taken into account when determining how long to cook it. I tried my hand with a slice as the waitress in the pink apron watched attentively, her black almond eyes benevolently willing me to succeed. Under the gaze of such beauty not only did my culinary skills feel on trial, but also my manhood, my desirability and – as I inevitably lost control of my piece of beef in the murky depths of the broth – the West itself. By the time I had fished around and secured the meat between my chopsticks, it had the consistency of shoe leather. She laughed sweetly in the contrived baby voice which girls in Japan are taught from adolescence – infinitely consoling to most Japanese men, but, under the circumstances, hardly conducive to my own confidence. Even after a couple of hours of experimentation, I failed to prepare anything as good as she had cooked me; nor did Masamichi or Yuki get it quite right. And even if our culinary skills had enabled us to do justice to such fabulously fresh and exquisite in-gredients, we might still have asked ourselves whether $1,400 for three could be said to represent value for money. Though the perfection of the food, the service, and even the building somehow seemed to compensate for the shabby chaos of Shinjuku, we departed shocked and a little gloomy into the warm, late autumn evening.

Overhead the moon stood like a sentry looking down unperturbed on this frantically restive district, which seemed to be on permanent heat. Masamichi led us confidently around corners, into clusters of side streets, back onto a boulevard, and finally to a square building on a corner which seemed to have a "private club" on every floor.

"So, please go up," he said, directing me to a narrow, winding staircase covered by a nasty mauve carpet, his outstretched arm ordering me to proceed. As I followed his instructions, a taxi swiftly drew up and swallowed Yuki into its dark interior. She submitted to this abduction as if it were standard procedure. Her face had that perfect composure that Westerners mistakenly call "inscrutable".

"Where's she going?" I called to Masamichi from halfway up the first flight of stairs, dismayed.

"Home," he barked dismissively, waving goodbye to the taxi as if banishing it from the scene. He must have hailed it while I wasn't looking.

"I haven't even said goodnight," I replied in a plaintive tone. Her sudden disappearance had a touch of violence to it. I felt robbed of her, and anxious that she might think I'd been in on her undignified dispatch to her lonely marital bed. I stomped unenthusiastically up the stairs, increasingly melancholic about the matter-of-fact brutality of men's treatment of women – the groper in the train, Masamichi's discarding of Yuki without allowing me to extend her a goodbye or even a smile, the industrial scale of the sex industry in Shinjuku, with its legions of compliant girls and bossy *mama-sans*, all feverishly geared to men's demands for gratification. Even my memory of the lovely waitress with the baby voice and the expert way with *shabu-shabu* got on my nerves.

Masamichi herded me to the fifth floor – where the spectacle that greeted us beggared belief.

As always with the Japanese sex industry, the breathtaking

element was the casual mix of brazenness and innocence, of the outrageous and the unselfconscious. Masked men on all fours were being shoved around by "hostesses" dressed in black leather corsets with latex accessories and stiletto heels. The women, wielding hot candles, pokers and whips, shouted abuse at their bleating clients. Some of the customers had been saddled and were being ridden around the room, directed this way and that with strokes of the whip and withering insults. One man wearing a mask of a female deity was collapsing under the weight of two women, an Asian and a Western blonde, who were fondling each other as they meted out heavy blows to their squealing charge. Other clients in metal-studded dog collars were barking and scratching like crazed hounds as they were brutally pulled on straining leashes.

I felt a hand gently grip my elbow. While I watched a nearly nude middle-aged man being beaten with a heavy rubber dildo, an off-duty dominatrix was firmly leading me to a couch beneath the iron grills of what appeared to be a medieval dungeon. She twittered something into my deafened ears, which was presumably intended to put me at my ease, but I understood nothing.

"This place must be very unusual?" I said to Masamichi, trying to look as if I were enjoying the "entertainment" that was probably costing him even more than the *shabu-shabu*. "In most places like this, isn't it men beating women?"

"Maybe so," he said, "but what's the difference?"

The difference, I thought, was obvious: though the women were doing the beating, and hamming up their brutality, they were still letting themselves be used. But this was hardly the time to argue the toss with Masamichi.

I looked around warily. The opposite side of the dim emporium was dominated by a huge phosphorescent crucifix tied by ropes to large nails in the crimson wall. Tall candles stood like glowing sentries on either side of it, dripping red wax onto a carpet, like blood stains. Another wall had "Moulin Rouge" scrawled over it at a dozen different angles.

As the obligatory scotch on the rocks was placed in my hand by some semi-clad harridan, I did my best to seem comfortable in this unexpected atmosphere.

"Are you a member here?" I yelled at Masamichi, trying to be heard above the din of screams and heavy metal.

"No, no. Another Rotary Club member arranged tonight," he shouted back. "For you. In honour of you. Western guests expect such side of Japan, so I determine to show you, for the sake of your education. But this is very special place for you; you very privileged to be here."

It's true that most Western visitors feel deprived of the real Japan if they don't encounter its shadowy side, its sex shows, where the cruder human instincts are on exuberant display. Even the most sober and upright foreigners feel short-changed if they haven't dipped a toe into such dark waters, if only as non-participating voyeurs. The shows are irresistible spectacles partly because they contrast so comically with Japan's refined restraint, and partly because they seem as integral to Japanese culture as temples, tea ceremonies and kimonos, almost as if the one balanced the other.

A stifled shout suddenly issued from the man being ridden by two women; as one of them gripped him round the throat and pulled up the lower part of his mask, the other stuffed a huge dummy into his protesting mouth. He reared like a horse as they brought their crops down on him with extra ferocity, laughing and grimacing like the triumphant sadists he had paid them to be. They thrashed him in perfect synchrony.

"How about I order a Buddhist nun for you?" Masamichi asked mischievously. "Under robes she dressed as vampire."

I bashfully declined.

"So you prefer more soothing things: a milkshake?"

A "milkshake" turned out to be a breastfeeding service in which men in nappies can suckle on lactating women while feigning baby noises. The way Masamichi explained it, customers could choose between "suckling" or "mother's touch".

"Suckling is sucking the tit," he explained helpfully, "both tit if you like. Mother's touch, that comes after suckling the tit, she pat you and whisper and make you feel sleepy. And give you the tit. You like it?" he exclaimed, expansively, gesturing at the violent and obscure fantasies being played out all around us. "You happy? You know what big privilege for you to be here?"

"Sure," I said, assuming he was being ironic.

"Big privilege. Did you see notice on door?"

"No?"

"Special care taken to arrange this for you. My business colleague, Sato-san, specially arranged for you. He really like you."

I can't say I was flattered. I dimly remembered Sato-san from a buffet dinner organized by Masamichi's local Rotary Club chapter, to which Masamichi had finally gained admission after years of grovelling to its septuagenarian leaders. Sato was a big, affluent, jocular figure, a walking mosaic of designer labels who laughed chestily, and a little spookily, out of his gold- and silver-filled mouth. He chaired the Rotary chapter's social committee, which met every Friday afternoon and organized weekly lunches, golfing trips to Hawaii and weekends in prosperous resorts like Karuizawa, an hour north of Tokyo by bullet train. Come to think of it, I could imagine Sato ordering a "milkshake" for himself, and even a few lashes of the whip for dessert.

By the time we got up to leave Sato's club, the loud debauchery was no longer able to smother my gathering blues. I was filled by intense loneliness, by an overwhelming urge for the reassurances of the mundane. These feelings gave a new lustre to the thought of the everyday sights and sounds waiting for me on the street outside, conferring great powers of consolation on their banalities and obligations. It occurred to me that Japanese men might undergo such bizarre public rituals as I'd just seen not merely to fulfil their darker needs, but also to refresh their appetites for the ordinary. Perhaps they needed this sort of thing to mock the enslavement of corporate life, or to experience it as intoxicating rather than as numbing, as well as to renew their combat-readiness for its unrelenting pressures.

The door closed behind us, relief swept through me, and we retraced reassuring steps back down the stairs. As we turned a corner, I saw a hand-scrawled sign advertising the club's presence, and at last understood the great efforts that Masamichi must have gone to in setting up my visit. The biggest letters on the sign warned: ONLY JAPANESE ADMISSION.

14

SHADOW LIFE

The Japanese soul resembles the Japanese house: its bare structure is austere and simple; its expressive richness can be evoked only in dim illumination; and if you were to direct a spotlight at it, you would conceal rather than reveal its essence.

At first, I found it hard to live in my tiny, traditional-style house. Not because of its practical challenges, such as brushing the *tatami* mats, remembering not to stick my fists through the *shoji* doors' paper panes, or sitting for long periods on the floor. Rather, its dim and empty space disoriented me. Like most Westerners, I am used to my home being filled with light and objects. In the West, we love brightness for its own sake and for the way it brings our dwellings to life. And we need our objects, however spare or sleek their design, as markers that give meaning to space and relief to its emptiness.

In traditional Japanese houses, the reverse is true. Dimness, not brightness, brings the rooms to life. And empty space, silent space, is the animating quality. The most poetic objects in the room – a ceramic vase or a hanging scroll or staggered shelves – usually hug the walls or are set back in alcoves. These constraints are dictated by Japanese architecture itself and the centuries-old sensibility which nourishes it. You can't overcome them by thinking to yourself, "Damn it, I'm just going to fill my rooms with books and chairs, and lighten them with tastefully discreet lamps, and then I'll feel at home." If you do this, the objects will look ungainly and out of place. The excess lighting will make the *fusuma* partitions and mud-plastered walls look flimsy and dowdy. Everything, from paper panes to lacquer, will appear too garish and obvious. The brightness will violate the room's pristine proportions.

You even need to be careful how you let in the sun. If you just throw open the *shoji*, the sunlight flooding the interior will put the shadows to flight and banish all the magic. Direct sunlight overwhelms rather than illuminates; in particular, it obscures one of the most beautiful aspects of the Japanese house, the patina of *tatami* and of the soft wood that frames and criss-crosses the *shoji*. Indeed, white, brilliant light seldom reveals what is most quintessentially Japanese, whether in architecture, gardens, landscapes, lacquer, the Noh stage, or other embodiments of the national spirit. Even the early-evening sun is altogether too radiant to evoke their layers of silent presence.

Much more appropriate illumination is afforded by moonlight, and its muted, silvery rays. Just attend the superb moon-viewing ceremony, usually performed in October: it captures the essence of Japan more than any sunrise or even sunset, let alone a midday sun. Dawn or dusk over Mount Fuji is grandiose, not least because of the mountain's wondrous symmetry and its magical solitude, but dawn and dusk are impressive in many mountainous parts of the world. There's something about moonlight – shining on, say, a garden or temple or *tatami* room – that is more singularly Japanese:

the matt, unshowy, indirect beams, sombre without being gloomy; the way the moon tempers the brute force of the sun; the mercurial border between night and day; the clarity interpolated by layers of opacity; the mood of yearning and serenity. It's a bit like the way in which black-and-white photographs can capture the essence of things better than colour. In this sense, the Japanese are truly people of the moon.

How odd, then, that this country is called the land of the rising sun. Or that the Japanese claim ancestry from the Sun Goddess. Perhaps they define themselves by the sun, which is in every sense an origin – of the nation, of its light, of its energy – because an origin is easier to grasp, to name, to describe, than the complex present. And because defining an origin cannot destroy it. Whereas the present, though closer to hand, is too immediate, too diverse, too fleeting, to be encapsulated in a single myth; any clear definition of it would violate its very nature which – particularly in Japan, is to be ambiguous, intangible, shadowy.

I am suggesting, in other words, that the way the Japanese identify their nation with an origin, the Sun and the Sun Goddess, has the inestimable benefit of releasing the present, as far as possible, from the straitjacket of crude simplifications and falsifications upon which all self-interpretation depends. Such release is feasible because the present is always to some extent independent of its sources, in that it cannot be entirely explained or justified by them. The instinctive desire, which pervades Japan, to defend the innocence of the now, to protect the inescapable vagueness of the present from the violence of definitions, is for me one of the most magnificent – and maddening – elements in the elusive Japanese soul.

15

FIRE WITH FIRE

For years I had dreamed of spending *Oshogatsu*, or New Year, in Kyoto, the ancient capital of Japan, where tradition and modernity collide with each other like nowhere else in the country.

I was met at the hideous main station – an eyesore almost as bad as the adjacent "Kyoto Tower" – by my German friend, Sophie, whom I'd encountered in Berlin a few months beforehand. She was wonderfully humane, took delight in wit and badinage, and relished her food. She astonished the locals with her loud laugh, her ultra-solid build, her fluent Japanese, and the long mane of wavy blond hair that framed her wide face and blue eyes and splashed down over her broad shoulders. Her diminutive boyfriend Toshie was in tow, a twice-divorced man considerably her senior who called her "Barbie" all evening – or "Baby", as I realized much later. Either variant seemed singularly inappropriate for this imposing Valkyrie.

We wended our way out of the station, past some stalls blaring out 'Silent Night' and 'Rudolf the Red-Nosed Reindeer', and past a Santa Claus in full regalia who, a week after Christmas, was still bellowing incitements and promises

103

to invisible little children. Jumping into Sophie's beat-up
Honda, we headed straight for a wine shop in a distant
suburb, where the store owner proudly showed us two large
albums containing the labels of every outstanding wine he
had ever drunk – a list of great Bordeaux and Burgundy and
Rhône that would make any wine buff green with envy.
Armed with a couple of wonderful bottles, we drove on to
dinner at the house of Sophie's close friend Emi, a Japanese-
American who had come to Japan to discover her roots and
"do tea", as studying the intricate practice and philosophy
of the tea ceremony is known among the cognoscenti. The
other guests, both of them Japanese, were a shy student – an
ardent admirer of Sophie's, whose quiet passion for her had
only intensified with every rejection – and a gardener with
a crew cut and a wicked glint in his eye, whose infallibly
successful party act was a tiramisu more delicious than any
I had eaten in Italy.

"Professor at Todai?" chuckled the gardener sardonically.
"Professor at Todai," and at once he collapsed into hysterical
laughter, rolling over onto his back on the sofa on which he
had been lounging, and shaking his legs in the air. Gardeners
in Japan, and especially in Kyoto, the Mecca of the classical
Japanese garden, are regarded as artists of the highest order; this
one clearly relished the privileges that went with his status.

"What's so funny about Todai?" Sophie asked him,
embarrassed for me.

"Nothing, nothing," he stammered, still convulsing with
laughter.

I really didn't get this at all. Laughter in Japan often
signals a refusal or an inability to engage with something.
Was there something about Todai, or me, that he found
ridiculous, inaccessible, intimidating, incomprehensible, irrelevant, dangerous? Or all of these?

The gardener calmed down for a moment, then turned to look at me again and sank back into helpless laughter. "Oh, just snap out of it," Emi barked at him in English, as she brought in a bowl of piping-hot *spaghetti alle vongole*. She repeated herself in Japanese, impatient, though unsurprised, at his behaviour.

The gardener summoned a little composure, stared at me as if I were some strange misfit from the pages of Grimm's fairy tales and exclaimed sententiously:

"Ah, Todai! Japan best university. And Japan worst university. Clever students. But wrong results. Wrong for Japan. Wrong for our future."

I couldn't have put it more succinctly myself after nine months in the place.

"Best people in Japan are ordinary nature people," he continued in a serious vein, obviously with himself in mind. "Workers, farmers, craftsmen, chefs. They have real sense of things. Exceptional understanding of the universe. They don't make financial mistakes of Todai people. Todai supply top officials of Ministry of Finance and big banks. These people get Japan into terrible mess. Ordinary people understand commands of universal bank manager. They understand real world money, not Todai world finance."

This all made good enough sense, except that I couldn't for the life of me figure out who the universal bank manager was. Such a cosmic executive had certainly never deigned to advise me on my finances. I asked the gardener at which branch he could be found.

"He is everywhere," he responded solemnly. "He regulates all business. Everything become balanced with him. He always provide money when really needed, when can be paid back. And he refuse loans when too much."

The odd thing was that he wasn't jesting. For him, the Buddhist principle of cosmic harmony really seemed to find embodiment in an all-wise bank manager. One only had to understand the basic principles of financial harmony for all to be well with Japan. Only the over-educated had lost contact with this reality.

He was still lying on the sofa, having declined to join us at the table. After a while he fell silent, staring vacantly at the ceiling, and a couple of minutes later was fast asleep. His brief oration over, he had opted out of the evening. The student playfully patted his bristly, somnolent head, as if dismissing his antics and his opinions as merely eccentric. Underneath, however, the student seemed curious how I'd coped – whether I'd shrugged the attack off or been humiliated. During my first month in Japan all that strange laughter would have thrown me. But by now I was used to being either venerated or mocked. *Gaigin*, especially when they occupy a position that the Japanese themselves recognize as prestigious, can be subject to daftly inflated respect (highly unsettling stuff), or to sudden ridicule at moments when their oddities seem especially conspicuous or inept. The ridicule, like the respect, is seldom merited. But of the two, by far the more perilous is the respect, because it imperceptibly frees you from those daily challenges to personal identity without which we fail to mature and evolve. Which is one reason why a short stay in Japan refreshes your life with a slew of new perspectives, while a long time there can regress it into a sort of perpetual adolescence.

"It's nearly nine!" Emi shouted, as I was helping myself to a third plate of spaghetti. "We've got to go right away!"

"Go where?"

"To see the lighting of the fires on Mount Daimonji. They're lit at nine and last only around fifteen minutes."

The girls quickly changed into kimonos. We abandoned our pasta, grabbed the gardener's tiramisu, piled into two cars and sped off.

Sophie explained that this ceremony normally took place only in August, at the time of *Obon*, the great annual festival for the dead, when the spirits of the deceased are believed to visit the earth for a couple of weeks before returning to their invisible lands. But this year it was to be repeated on New Year's Eve. The fires on the mountainside would trace the outline of the Chinese character for "big" or "great".

We left the cars at a small parking lot and clambered up a long flight of stone steps to a row of old wooden houses perched on the side of a hill opposite the mountain. Sophie's young admirer brought up the rear, dragging his gaunt limbs, shivering in the cold winter air, and sticking close to her boyfriend. He was oppressively private, though fixated on his unattainable love.

The house we entered, which belonged to an absent friend of Emi, seemed even colder inside than out. We knelt by a large open window, wrapped in coats and any blankets we could find, and waited for the silhouetted mountain to spring to life. At precisely nine, the brooding mass was illuminated by a single fire. Its slope, which had looked deserted in the dark, suddenly swarmed with tiny human figures. Other fires followed in quick succession, tracing a complex path that eventually formed the complete character. The scene flared brightly for around ten minutes before slowly dying out, restoring the mountain to its dark privacy. So that was the festival of *Daimonjiyaki* – of "burning Daimonji"! Somehow, it all seemed too brief, too pointless, too contrived, an ancient custom still respected in the form but, as so often in today's Japan, stripped of its power to evoke the presence of spirits, gods, or kind fates. An acute sense of emptiness filled the room.

Then, from next door, raunchy pop lyrics boomed into the freezing night and through the flimsy walls of our room. Prince was feeling horny and didn't mind who knew about it, and his lust-addled refrain "you sexy motherfucker" was resonating through the old wooden house.

After the elegiac, dried up drama of burning Daimonji, Prince seemed shocking. But not infuriating. Perhaps his blunt paean to sexual gratification was *so* out of place in this traditional house and ancient city that it couldn't even jar with them.

"That must be Hideo," said Emi, laughing with typical exuberance. "He shares this floor of the house." She flung open a door, revealing a young man reclining with two demonically seductive girls under halos of cigarette smoke.

Hideo gave us a look as cursory as it was dismissive. Since the girls' languid gazes followed Hideo's attention wherever it went, I inevitably fell into their eroticized field of vision. Like countless other *gaigin* confronted by delicious Japanese femininity, I was briefly and pathetically unable to resist the illusion that they might have detected in me the elemental masculinity that had so far eluded them, or that they had sensed a hidden promise of freedom and wealth that only a Western man could fulfil. But such hopes would have been futile: contrary to mythology, Japanese women usually prefer Japanese men – even if they find a Western boyfriend a useful short-term accessory. Few, if any, are Madame Butterflies who live to serve and submit in every conceivable way. Nor are they all stifled prisoners of male chauvinism panting for rescue by the egalitarian Westerner and his shining platinum card.

Nonetheless, the lustre of the evening went up when the three of them suggested that we all attend the great fire festival in the centre of town before going on to ring the temple bells at midnight.

We filed back down the long stone steps, the girls giggling as their high heels got stuck between the uneven slabs, and pretending to be perilously unbalanced. Their feline gait rippled with sexual tension, part real and part mocking, as they undulated their hips and flung their hair around their snow-white necks. I suspected they viewed our party as amusingly quaint and sexless: Emi, the American in kimono, spending years learning how to drink a cup of tea; Sophie, with her passion for Japanese lacquerware; her antiquated boyfriend, Toshie, with his old-fashioned haircut and the trademark facial tic of the overworked salaryman; the perpetually unrequited student, sticking closely to Toshie's side out of love for Sophie, instead of ploughing more promising soils; and me, a *gaigin* philosopher at Todai, whatever that is… Like many younger Japanese, they laughed quite openly – though without spite or mockery – at whatever they found quirky and hidebound.

In the square outside Kyoto's City Hall, thousands of people were packed shoulder to shoulder, many climbing up lamp-posts or onto the roofs of kiosks and subway exits to get a better view of the massive fire blazing in the centre. There were parades and bands, troupes of half-naked male dancers wielding huge torches, and swarms of people making merry all around. The enormous screen onto which all this was projected was itself only half-visible, and we couldn't get very close to the action: the borders of the vast crowd were impenetrable. All I could see were trails of sparks shooting up into the air like so many little comets, then evaporating into the dark night. All I could hear above the din of revellers and announcements was the drone of invisible policemen yelling instructions through their megaphones.

Presently, a parade that was marching around the square abruptly stopped, the crowd calmed down, and a man in a business suit popped onto the giant screen and began a speech. It was about peace, and had all the electricity of a slug sliding across a slab of stone. In Japan speeches are almost invariably boring, but speeches about peace are downright intolerable. Of course, one ought to have been thankful that Japan had become such a genuinely peace-loving nation, such a model international citizen. But the sentiments and phrases of Japanese pacifism are so deadeningly mechanical that they snuff the life out of remembrance. They are churned out by a state-led peace industry, as if the nation is perpetually brainwashing itself into tranquillity. Memory is, after all, an odd thing, and often not best-served by rituals of commemoration.

This was certainly the moment to move on, especially as we were unlikely to get any closer to the action. But it was only ten-fifteen and, with so much time to spare before midnight, Emi suggested we visit the monastery where she had started studying tea. The abbot there was a laugh a minute, she claimed, a lech, an expert on Chinese love poetry, a master of the tea ceremony, and a devotee of heavy metal into the bargain. He sounded irresistible.

16

THE ART OF ZEN MATING

The Abbot greeted us as if he had been expecting our visit all along, and even in the dimly lit entrance hall I was struck by his dignified, no-nonsense bearing. Humane and hard, humble and masterful, his seemingly contradictory traits were fused into a powerful and harmonious character. As a result, his presence was protective, but didn't allow you to hide. It was tolerant, but didn't allow anyone to be phoney. It was embracingly warm, but bracingly strict. Above all, it was alert – alert with a degree of precision, clarity, intensity, and unsentimental compassion that merited the over-used epithet "spiritual". A magnificent man!

He beckoned us into his reception room, where two Westerners, an Australian girl and an American man, were sipping sake and helping themselves to a suite of delicacies lined up on the *tatami*. The Australian girl, pretty but slightly heavy-limbed, with long, sleek black hair, was studying for a doctorate on the history of *Onsens*, the volcanic spas dotted all over the country – a cushy dissertation topic if ever I'd heard of one. The American was just the sort of Western Zen Buddhist that you expected to meet in Kyoto: a 1960s ex-hippy from a well-to-do family, who had manned the student barricades in '68, dropped out of Berkeley, come to Japan all those years ago, trained in this monastery and never left. One could imagine him in the Sixties, reading Zen poems on acid before upping sticks for Japan. He was tense and gaunt, and exuded nervy suffering – suffering that he had controlled but not mastered, despite his practised art of appearing laid-back.

"Come, I'll prepare you some *matcha* green tea," said the abbot in excellent English, taking my arm and leading me to a small corner of the long room.

"Go on, that's a real honour," whispered Sophie, sensing my embarrassment about the abbot himself preparing the tea.

"Sure it is!" chuckled the abbot, overhearing her.

I sat down on the floor while he prepared the tea with immaculate precision but utterly relaxed informality. It was a far cry from all those starchy demonstrations of the tea ceremony that I had witnessed since arriving in Japan.

"You can't imagine how tough it is doing tea like that," Emi cooed. "I've been learning it for three years now, and I still look either clumsy or over-formal. You have to understand all the associated arts, like lacquer, scrolls and calligraphy, to become as expert as he is."

He presented me the bowl of *matcha* with a bow, whose absolute correctness sent Emi to the second level of swooning, then lost no time in getting down to basics.

"So what's your field of philosophy?"

"Ethics and German Idealism."

"Mmm. OK. Japanese are very attracted to German Idealism. We like its darkness; its shadowy, mystical, ecstatic element; its romantic feeling for nature; its resistance to an objective world of light and clarity. But do you think the nineteenth-century Idealists – excepting Kant, of course – made any lasting contribution to ethics?"

As we debated, I warmed to the abbot's erudition for its humanity as much as for its depth. He was no dry scholar. For him philosophy raised the supreme question of how to live a worthwhile life, and he had used his extensive knowledge of Eastern and Western thought to investigate it. And I loved the way he spoke his mind, so clearly and modestly; the slow simplicity with which he inspected his own assumptions; his tough-minded realism – the purity and intensity and discipline of which again struck me as "spiritual", indeed as defining features of the spiritual.

"And your love life? How often have you really been in love?" he demanded abruptly, shearing away from our arcane topic to leave me gaping and unable to reply. "My dear boy," he taunted, "you've never really been in love. I can see that! Or not more than once, I'd say. But one love does not make a life any more than one swallow makes a summer." He seemed quite proud of this turn of phrase. "Come over here," he said, pointing to the Australian. "She's a lovely girl. Just enjoy her, don't think about whether she's right for you. But if you don't like her, you might like this one!" And he fished from under his robes a photograph of a stunning Japanese girl posing provocatively in kimono. His eyes were shining with mischief.

"Why don't I go straight for that one?" I whispered, pointing at the dazzling picture.

"OK, I'll call her then. Her mother's on the lookout for the right man. What makes you think you're the one for her?" Then *sotto voce*: "Go and talk to the sweet Australian while I call her. You know our Zen saying: 'Let go of your wits and become like a ball in a mountain torrent'. Discipline is no good without letting go! Don't hesitate. *Stop* hesitating!"

I hesitated, concerned that I was getting myself into more hot water than I needed to. Though the abbot was a tease, his subtext was serious.

"You're surprised Zen abbots behave this way?" he said, reading my mind. "Most Westerners don't understand Zen mentality. We are very strict. But also very light-hearted. Controlled, but also spirited. True to reality, but also full of fantasy. In all cases, we can only build the second on top of the first. It took *him* years to understand what that really means," he said pointing a tad dismissively at the American chatting to Sophie.

The American, who had obviously been eavesdropping, immediately butted in, his demeanour both curious and defensive:

"Most foreigners who come here to do Zen don't ever do it properly," he agreed. "They're attracted to Zen because it's free of systems and doctrines. But, in practice, they can't cope with that freedom. They go on craving explanations and quick fixes for the problems of life, as well as a good dose of mysticism, though Zen provides none of that. And they get irritated by the hard discipline – by the fact that nothing can be left to chance if you're ever to become spontaneous. Even to sit properly takes years of practice – helped, of course, by the fear of getting whacked with a long wooden stick if your posture slips. Sooner or later, most of them say, 'Fuck this, man, I'm out of here! These monks are fucking maniacs'." And he laughed a spooky, triumphant, questioning laugh.

"You've been here since 1968?" I asked.

"Since 1970," interjected the abbot condescendingly. "I told him to move on. You can get too comfortable in a single monastery."

"I don't know about comfort," said the American. "What

with getting up every morning at 4 a.m. to read sutras, meditate, scrub flagstones, sweep leaves, weed the garden." He was just getting into his stride when he became pensive. "Anyway, I had this really tough problem. I got cancer of the kidney three years ago, went back to the States to get operated, got stuffed with chemotherapy, and then they told me I had six months to live. But I'm still here, and the reason I'm alive is this place and what it's taught me."

The abbot's face looked tautly benevolent, and also a little impatient.

"They couldn't believe it in the States," he continued. "You know, my Dad's a retired professor of medicine. I had the best doctors and surgeons. You can't get better cancer treatment anywhere in the world. But those guys don't understand why I'm still around. Nor do I really, except that it's either Zen or a miracle, and I'm inclined to believe it's Zen."

This remarkable story went some way towards explaining the American's skeletal appearance, and the sense that his life was balanced on a knife-edge. But it didn't explain everything about the bitter gravity of his eyes and the confused self-pity that seemed to menace his spirit. There was something very Western in that look, something you would hardly encounter in a Japanese – even one with worse afflictions. What was Western was the refusal, beyond a very limited point, to deal with fate; an expectation of some guaranteed minimum level of happiness in life, and an inability to master disappointment when it isn't attained. From such disappointment flow festering regrets, resentments and feelings of injustice. This clutch of feelings is profoundly alien to the Japanese spirit – and especially to that intense distillation of it found in Zen. This Japanese way doesn't try to gild or soften the blows of fate by ascribing to them elevated meanings or hidden blessings, and can seem atrociously cruel. So the Westerner in Japan, however hostile he thinks he is to the values of his homeland, can quickly find himself screaming into a vast, silent desert, isolated and unheard and depersonalized.

I was about to ask more questions of the American when the Abbot again interjected:

"I said before that the time for philosophizing is over. Now is the time for love! Time to be an idiot! Please be an idiot, or you will never learn to think!" And with that classic instruction of the Zen master, he flung his arm over my shoulder, dragged me over to the Australian girl and sat me down at her side. She had heard this summons, and looked distinctly sheepish.

"Couple," he instructed us, then left the room, perhaps to telephone the beauty in the kimono.

For a moment or two we both looked coyly around us. Hideo and his girls had settled down with the student and were having a roaring time, aided by large quantities of sake. Sophie was muttering something to an indifferent-looking Toshie, who – half listening and half self-absorbed – was replying "Yes Barbie" where appropriate.

"Are many abbots like this?" I asked, breaking into the silence and reaching for one of the delicacies lined up on the floor, a shiny rice cake surrounded by sweetened red beans. I enjoyed feeling its squashy consistency.

"They don't all have the erudition, but most have the clarity and directness. Behind the humour, there's tremendous seriousness of purpose. Behind the banter, they are men of few words, real straight talkers."

"I get the sense that he's astonished how hard people find it to enjoy life, rather than to snatch a pleasure here and there."

"That's it. There's a whole discipline to enjoyment," she said. "A whole set of skills. They believe that you've got to be very rigorous, spare and precise in your life in order to enjoy it. But those virtues aren't illuminated by studying texts, as they are in other Buddhist sects or in Judaism, Islam and Christianity. In fact, they believe that texts and concepts get in the way of relating to reality."

"I've noticed that in the philosophy department at Tokyo University," I said, in all seriousness. "This is definitely not a philosophical country. Systems, speculation, 'grasping' the world – in both senses of that word – are alien to the Japanese."

"Yes, for them, the world is discovered through action, not through concepts."

"Speaking of action, are these monks lecherous? Have you ever seen them bring women here or go down to the red-light district?"

"I've seen women literally trying to break in here," she said. "Some women are powerfully attracted to monks, especially to their strength of mind. Purity of purpose turns them on. And of course, some of the monks are pretty lusty – though probably no more so than monks in Europe have been for centuries. But not the abbot: in his youth maybe, but not any more – whatever the rumour mill might say."

"We should meet up tomorrow to…" But I was getting stuck in mid-sentence; not awkwardly, out of shyness, but literally; the rice cake I was trying to eat had glued my tongue to my upper palate and, far from breaking down under chewing, actually became more viscous. The wretched mass stuck like a leech to whatever it touched; and my tongue and swallowing muscles – which are surprisingly difficult to move in sync – could neither manoeuvre it forwards nor drag it backwards down my gullet. Trying to fix up an evening out with a newly met woman is not an easy task at the best of times; it's even harder when a little piece of rice cake has lodged at the back of your mouth and won't shift. I was coughing convulsively as I spoke, and quickly passed from embarrassment to worrying that I was about to choke to death. No matter how hard I tried to cough it out, I couldn't, and the only solution was to haul it out manually.

Everyone laughed as they saw my beetroot face and tear-stained eyes and fingers covered with the unbecoming gelatinous goo. It was the nearest I'd ever come to suffocating.

"Welcome to *mochi*," said Sophie, "symbols of long life and good fortune. They traditionally kill a few people every New Year's Eve."

Hearing the desperate gurgles of my near-death experience, the Abbot returned. "Oh, please take care! *Mochi* is sacred for us. We associate it with purity."

I thought he must be joking again. But he wasn't. This lethal mass of glutinous, pummelled rice is indeed sacred in Japan. *Mochi* manias have sprung up regularly in Japanese history. I've heard it said that in the eighth century the craze for *mochi* got so out of hand that too many labourers choked to death on it, threatening the entire economy with rice shortages, and forcing Prince Shotoku to ban it. Unfortunately, this attempt at prohibition, like most others in history, quickly failed, since any self-respecting sumo wrestler is capable of pounding rice into *mochi* cakes, and all adequate physiques were co-opted into producing them behind closed doors. The rage had to die a natural death, perhaps by killing its most fervent devotees.

Surely nothing is more mysterious than what human beings choose to make sacred.

"Tomorrow, 7 p.m., here," the Abbot told me, with a

wickedly victorious wink, ignoring my dishevelled condition.

"Sorry, I'm taken," I said, glancing at the Australian girl.

"You're too slow with these things."

"*Good!*" he exclaimed enthusiastically. "I thought you were the slow one."

An elderly maid came in with bowls of hot soup on a tray.

"Just before midnight on New Year's Eve we traditionally have this sort of soup," the abbot said. "*Toshi-koshi soba*" – literally "year-passing" noodle soup. "It's full of special noodles for long life! There's a bowl for each of you."

It was just what I needed after my perilous struggle with the rice cake. The bowl was made of the finest lacquer, and the sense of anticipation was exquisite as I impatiently removed the lid – which tugged a little against the suction cleaving it to the moist rim – and submitted to the wisps of aromatic vapours as they warmly caressed my face. We took our time inhaling its gentle scents, enjoying the sight of freshly chopped vegetables, shiny cubes of tofu, and perfectly formed shiitake mushrooms, savouring the first sips, and lazily following the steam's jagged ascent.

"My God, it's eleven-thirty," Sophie shouted, when our bowls were nearly empty, "we've got to go! There'll be a long line at Daitoku-ji monastery to ring the bells."

"Yes, we're off," said Emi, then in an aside to me: "The abbot's very hospitable, but I don't want to overstay our welcome."

The abbot bade us a farewell as brisk and dignified as his greeting. In Japan, goodbyes can be surprisingly snappy, free from the drawn-out assurances of gratitude and reunion common to leave-taking in the West. "If you want to meet the other one just call me," he confided, as I put on my shoes.

"See you tomorrow," I called to the Australian girl, as I winked back at him non-committally.

It was just as well we left then, because at least two hundred people were already standing in line outside the gates of the monastery at Daitoku-ji temple. This meant that the temple bell was going to be struck a lot more than the 108 times ordained by custom – 108 being the number of earthly desires that plague human nature, according to Buddhism, all of which are to be symbolically banished as the new year begins. It was also obvious that some people were having more than one crack at ringing the bell, presumably in the hope of achieving just the deep, sonorous sound needed to send these vices on their way.

After a few minutes standing impatiently in the freezing night air, there was a sudden upwelling of muted shouting and laughing and bowing: it was midnight. And there we were in this dark alley, shuffling to keep warm, a great misty wood to our left and the long monastery walls to our right, at the tail of an anonymous line of people, having reached nowhere in particular. We had slipped unknowingly into the New Year.

It took an hour and a half to get to the front of the line, and now I saw why it had been so long. You had to clamber up a narrow set of wooden stairs wide enough for only one person at a time, through a short tunnel – not a place for anyone with claustrophobia – and up onto a platform where a horizontal wooden log was suspended from the low ceiling by hemp ropes. Two monks helped you to grapple with it in your attempts to strike the great bronze bell. It wasn't easy: too much force and the bell gave out a harsh, grating clang; too little and it produced an insipid little squeak, hoarse and without resonance. The crisp winter air carried sound with exceptional clarity, and was merciless in exposing mediocrity. No wonder bell-ringing was a specialist business – in the old days, an occupation of its own. Your reward for the effort, however, no matter how unimpressive your results, was a tangerine doled out by another monk as you returned to the foot of the stairs.

It was about 1.30 in the morning now, and Toshie really wanted to get to bed, but Emi persuaded him to visit the nearby Imamiya shrine on our way home, where hundreds of people would already be gathering to bring New Year's offerings. And so they were. At the gates of the large compound were stalls where priests in white robes greeted us with sake and snacks and hot tea to sustain the long line of people that stretched to the main shrine, as little whiffs of steam and condensed breath rose over the snaking crowd like morning mist. Though few of the visitors looked animated by great religious zeal – most seemed to be observing the rites out of custom or mild superstition or as a social grace – the priests treated everyone with utmost kindness and acceptance. The whole compound was illuminated by a canopy of lanterns, between which families, monks, lovers and tourists meandered with tired, amiable contentment.

As I was wandering alone through a peripheral part of the complex containing some smaller shrines, I bumped into the Australian girl. She stood out next to a group of women in slightly kitschy flowered kimonos, their elfin necks encircled by elegant stoles on which their black hair buns daintily rested. I saw her from the side, throwing a coin into a box, clapping her hands and, eyes reverently closed, whispering a quick prayer – the ritual that most Japanese, whether religious or not, observe at shrines. It was odd to find a foreigner doing this so naturally.

She seemed delighted to see me, and at once fished into her bag and pulled out a white envelope. With mock seriousness, she presented it to me in good Japanese style with both hands and a bow and a snappy "*Hai dozo*". I couldn't read a word except her signature.

"It's your *nengajo* – your New Year's card. Let it be the year in which you stop dithering!"

"The abbot's obviously been having a word with you," I retorted.

"The abbot's not the only one who can see the obvious. Of course, we *have* just entered the year of the snake, the sort of year in which retiring philosophers in search of wisdom have an excuse to postpone other priorities."

This cheeky put-down really endeared her to me.

"Anyway, have you done *your* New Year's cards?"

"What New Year's cards? No, I haven't."

"Oh, that's a real black mark. In Japan you must send them to your colleagues and friends. The post office saves them up for the first of January, when it delivers the whole lot at the same time all over the country."

When I would return to my house in Kamakura three days later, sure enough I would find a heap of cards waiting for me, neatly tied into a bundle, many of them written with the awesomely disciplined spontaneity of traditional calligraphy.

"Let's stop dithering in the cold and go back to my place for a drink," she said.

We walked the mile or so back to her monastery, through silent streets deserted except for the odd clutch of revellers and parents dragging exhausted children to bed – the mothers in kimono walking with their short, constrained steps, while the fathers in traditional baggy *hakama* trousers and *haori* jackets strode ahead more freely and purposefully.

Just off the entrance hall to the monastery, the old maid sat at a little desk smiling through her crooked mouth and, with shaky but deft sweeps of her calligraphy brush, finishing her last New Year's cards. When we enquired after the abbot, she told us he was out partying and wouldn't return before 4 a.m. at the earliest.

All night we lay about drinking sake, chatting about Zen and failed love and nonsense, spread out on square cushions and *tatami* mats, until dawn broke on the first day of the new year.

17

How to Die

Snow was falling, and the crooked branches of the single cherry tree in my garden were laced with white. I lay decadently on my futon, watching the leisurely flakes zigzagging down like confetti, picking at the traditional New Year's delicacies that Miyako, my wonderful landlady, had brought me. Inside three square lacquer boxes, stacked one on top of the other, I found sticks of burdock root with sesame seeds, broiled lobster and sea bream, sweet steamed omelette squares, long boiled *daikon* radishes, salted herring roe, sweet black beans, dried sardines cooked in a sticky soy sauce, steamed fish paste, simmered arrowhead bulbs, pink fish cakes set in auspicious patterns, salmon rolled in kelp and tied with dried gourd, sweet marinated chestnuts, flower-shaped carrot roundels, seafood dressed with vinegar, pink-coloured jelly flavoured with plum wine and cut in the shape of a plum flower, pork roasted with soy sauce, and yellow-tail *teriyaki*... among other things. All this glorious fare supposedly symbolized long life and prowess, the seven-inch long radishes most obviously.

I nearly always photographed Miyako's food before diving into it – so beautifully was it prepared, with everything radiating freshness and beauty. But this morning I was too lazy even to fetch my camera from the drawer. My sole aim was to work my way through the pile of New Year's cards that had been waiting for me on my return from Kyoto the previous evening and, in essential cases, to whip off quick replies.

Odd: the only friends who hadn't sent me anything were Masamichi and Yuki. Though his free spirit was quite unpredictable, Masamichi always respected traditions of this sort. Had he found a new girlfriend, or come to grief in Shinjuku, or absconded abroad? I knew that he'd vanished from home for prolonged periods on two occasions, and had only been discovered with the aid of private detectives engaged by Yuki.

I doubted that he was offended with me: Japanese are seldom offended, at least not in that peevish way of many Westerners, which even a full apology can't erase. They might judge you a social misfit, or find you intolerable, or cut you from their lives and forget all about you. But unless you overtly insult them, their grievances seldom fester – another, most welcome, result of their amazing capacity to sanitize memory. (A telling paradox: cultures built on religions of forgiveness, notably Christianity and Islam, seem the most beset by gnawing resentment, the most unable to forget their hurts.)

I called him on his mobile to wish him a happy New Year, and found him inexplicably monosyllabic. Nothing I said elicited the slightest interest. This was unprecedented.

"Is everything really all right?" I finally ventured – not a question asked lightly in Japan, for fear that an untruthful yes or a truthful no will prove embarrassing... To cross such a threshold of privacy is a big step even between close friends.

"Absolutely fine. I always fine," he replied. "So," he said briskly, as though to shut me up, "how about dinner? Day after tomorrow OK for you?"

Masamichi never made appointments so far in advance, except with business colleagues. He prided himself on his spontaneity, and on having never possessed a diary or any sort of personal organizer. Something was going on.

"Friday's fine," I answered. "It's my treat. For New Year."

I called a restaurant that I knew he liked. Though I'd eaten there once before, I asked them to fax me a map. Tokyo backstreets look so similar that I could never find my way to tucked-away places, no matter how often I'd been to them. On the cover sheet of their reply they told me: "Dear Mr Lay, Thank you for your kind reservation. We are happily waiting to see you come." On the day itself, they sent another confirmation by fax: "We sincerely appreciate your reservation. At 8.00 p.m. we are expecting to see your come." And when I arrived on the night, the owner-cook declared his pleasure at my "second coming". They were nothing if not thorough.

The restaurant was hidden in an alley in Ebisu, one of my favourite areas of Tokyo, full of life but not as clichéd or self-conscious in its exuberance as, say, Ginza or Roppongi, which I found to be spooky, disembodied places, for all their perpetual motion. The food there was not at all ornate, but made from the freshest ingredients: baked lotus roots, asparagus with salty bean paste, juicy shiitake and *maitake* mushrooms, oyster tempura, crab cakes, and delicious sake in bamboo containers. Unusually, noodle soup was served first, and Masamichi slurped his soup down at record speed without saying a word, the long thick noodles vanishing into his mouth like flailing eels. He bent low over the bowl, in a posture of unreachable privacy, sucking and shoving its contents into his mouth, bowing his head each time as he did so, as if at prayer. Slurping your soup in this hectic, deliberately uncouth manner is *de rigeur* in Japan – even for women, who are otherwise required to eat without revealing the unseemly processes of chewing and swallowing. There might be more than a dozen angles at which to bow, and over ten ways of saying the word "I", but there is only one way of eating soup, and the more dramatic your sound effects the better. Enjoying it in leisurely silence, Western-style, is regarded as quite improper, while blowing it cooler is considered positively spineless.

Masamichi said nothing until he had polished off the whole bowl.

"By the way, my father's dying."

I tried not to look shocked, but I had to say something. "I'm so sorry, Masamichi. How absolutely awful."

"No need to be sorry. It's the will of the universe."

It turned out, however, that the will of the universe had been given a helping hand by the terrible medical treatment that his father had received for a long-standing cancer.

"There's no nursing after operation. We, the family, must do everything. Once hospital decides you are finished, you are finished. They leave patient to his family. So I go to clinic every day over New Year holiday. Situation not good."

I motioned to put my hand on his shoulder, less to offer him reassurance than to seduce him out of this bone-dry, staccato reportage, which I found quite unbearable. He recoiled from my touch, not by withdrawing but by stiffening his body and tightening his face, as though to squeeze the slightest hint of despondency out of himself. The idea of his crying on my shoulder, literally or otherwise, was inconceivable. Talking his way out of his grief was also difficult. He dealt with his anguish by ignoring it – the visible power of his discipline demonstrating the depth of his emotion.

"So! How about Kyoto? Beautiful temples? Beautiful women?"

I was galvanizing myself to give an amusing account of New Year, and to tickle him with stories of the Zen abbot and the Australian girl, when his mobile phone rang.

He looked very grave. He held his hand over the telephone to muffle his voice in a way that normally only Japanese women do.

"I must go immediately to hospital."

"I'll pay the bill and call you later," I said, resisting any hint of compassion.

"No, come with me. That'll be better. We need a philosopher!"

We left and drove over to the hospital. Masamichi was very, very preoccupied, but I knew by now to pretend not to notice, or to pretend not to show concern at what I noticed.

His father was half-absent in spirit, in the manner of terminally ill people, but surprisingly vigorous. He was laughing and looked relaxed, breezy and benevolent. He had a mop of tousled grey hair, small eyes set deeply in their sockets, a refined, symmetrical nose, bony arms and rather beautiful hands with long, tapered fingers. Despite his hoarse voice, he was talking and joking and even flirting with Masamichi's mother. She was a tiny, rotund lady with dyed black hair, bow legs typical of her generation, formidably strong eyes, and the same humorous twinkle as her son. It was immediately clear that she had been the boss in her long marriage. The room revolved around her rather than around the sick patient. As we entered, she fixed

Masamichi with a powerfully impassive stare, then her eyes
relaxed into warm, loving relief. There were decades in that
look. The son and the father greeted each other without
a hint of sadness or foreboding. The old man continued
chuckling at something that his wife had been saying. The
feeling of family was quite overpowering. This was like the
room of a convalescent, not of a dying man.

Masamichi said a few words to his father, then pulled his
mother over to introduce her. She was a fantastic character:
feisty, witty, resilient, warm and humane, despite everything
I had heard about the prejudice, verging on bigotry, that
she had inflicted on her daughter-in-law. There wasn't a
hint of weakness in the set of her mouth. Everything about
her face was direct, unsentimental, determined. In a few
minutes, she extracted a complete overview of my life, and
regaled me with stories of how she and her husband had
courted, married up in the Niigata mountains, and started
the architectural practice that Masamichi now ran. She told
me about the war, the firebombing, her love of Japanese
cinema, the first time she'd met a Westerner. But nothing
brought her so much to life as when I asked her if she was
proud of her son. She seized and hugged him:

"Maple!" she declaimed triumphantly.

"Maple?"

"Mayfly!" she said.

"Mayfly?"

Masamichi beamed like a delighted adolescent at these
attempts to say "My boy! My boy!" So much for Japanese
reserve.

We had been chatting in the corner of the room for no
longer than fifteen minutes when we heard a loud groan
from the bed, and swung about in alarm. Masamichi's
father was clutching the side of his head in agony. Then an

extraordinary thing happened. He raised both hands in the
air, waved at us, stared fervently, attempted a smile and – as
his arms fell to his side – collapsed into a coma. We rushed
over to the bed. His mouth was wide open, his cheeks
were alternately flushed and pale, and his breathing was
unfathomably deep, his chest rising and falling like a lifeboat
on the wild seas. Masamichi's normally taut face softened
into exquisite tenderness. His mother stared imploringly
at her struggling husband. Yuki was conspicuous by her
absence.

The death rattle began. For several dreadful minutes it
pummelled us with its furious, rhythmic, animal struggle.
Gradually, the intervals between the gasps became more
prolonged. The edges of his lips and the ridge of his nose
went a faint blue. And then he was dead.

For many moments time seemed to stop. No word
was uttered. No nurse or doctor came in. No look was ex-
changed between mother and son. The speed with which
everything had happened felt unreal: a moment ago, he
was alive and joking. Now he didn't exist. The tumour
in his brain might have abruptly burst, or a sudden stroke
finished him. In any event, the hospital staff seemed to have
concealed his true condition until they called Masamichi
over. And they obviously hadn't kept his mother informed
– she had just been so jaunty and talkative – unless she was
simply refusing to face reality.

It felt intrusive to stare at the body and its stiffening
mouth, or at the incredulous wife and son; so I let my eyes
wander over the dank, dingy room, quite the worst I have
ever seen in a hospital. The floor was part-carpeted with
dust, one of the walls was spattered with dried blood, and
paint was peeling off all the corners. Everything looked
flimsy and uncared for. And only now did I notice how

freezing the place was: the sole source of warmth was an ineffective fuel-powered stove spewing out noxious fumes. As so often in the Japanese winter, it seemed colder indoors than out. Yet I doubt these Spartan conditions had particularly bothered the old man. It's amazing what primitive quarters this prosperous, hygiene-obsessed, perfectionist people will tolerate. He was probably grateful for the modicum of privacy afforded by his pokey little box; being cooped up in a ward with two dozen other dying people would have been even worse.

A muffled whimper emerged out of the silence and presently broke into open wailing. Masamichi's mother was clutching her son with one arm and hugging the dreadfully unresponsive body with the other. The old man's face had filled out and suddenly acquired a younger, fresher, even boyish patina. The deep wrinkles, which only a few minutes earlier had furrowed the forehead and cheeks, had been almost wiped away. Disgust crept over me at the way Death mocked us by endowing that face with such plump shininess, instead of dispatching it instantly into the nothingness where it was headed.

As I wrestled with this thought, which refused every summons to depart, my mind was dragged back to a winter's evening in Moscow some ten years previously, when I had entered a dimly lit chapel in the Novodevichy Monastery. In a corner I found the body of an old woman in an open coffin. Her tiny, waxen face was crossed by a few delicate lines. The sight of her had filled me, for the first time, with the sublime élan of being alive when someone else is dead. Never before had I felt such gratitude for vitality and health, such exhilaration at how death made life real – as if death were the final proof of the almost unbelievable reality of existing. I felt awe at the genius of death in annulling decades of suffering for this woman in Soviet Russia's darkest days, under Stalin, the Nazi invasion, the KGB, purgers, betrayers and misanthropes of all kinds. All her suffering was now neatly stowed away in a corpse, sublimely impotent, beyond her own reach and that of the authorities. One day I would share her fate, but for now she was generously lying there in my stead. How horrifying empathy becomes with such a reaction: it acquires the hardness of the beast, the joy in safety of the torturer, the primal selfishness of the animal, the defiance of the victor – and yet one wouldn't want it any other way. One's conscience hurts, but it hurts only the reflective, genteel part of one's nature – not the will to live, not the will to prevail.

I was aroused from these morbid musings by a click of the door handle. A doctor and a grumpy nurse entered in a brisk, businesslike fashion, briefly extended condolences to the family, then examined the body. The doctor confirmed the death, and asked a few questions of Masamichi and his mother. Then Masamichi came over to me, his arm held around his mother protectively – the first time I had seen him do this to anybody, let alone a member of his family. I wanted to clasp her hand or hug her, but dreaded breaching the unknown conventions of Japanese death etiquette. She stared at me imploringly while her son, deeply moved by his father's dignified departure, asked me whether I now understood why the Japanese prided themselves on their "cheerfulness".

"You saw his wave," he said, fighting back tears. "This is how cheerful we are. Just say goodbye. That's it. Decisive. Joyful. Courageous. And no self-pity. This is Japan. In this, we are shining example to the world!"

Pride in father and country was now all that stood between him and desolation. Yet burning admiration for his father was scarcely something he had evinced before. On the contrary, he had seldom alluded to the old man, and then only as a bit of a loser, a weakling who had been unable to stand up to tough challenges, whether from his customers, his banks, or his wife. But now he was praising his father's qualities over and over again, identifying them with all that was best about Japan.

"For us Japanese, death is necessary stage before new life," he started again, trying to philosophize his way out of the moment. "New life on *this* earth," he added emphatically. "Western people always too sad about death, or console with heaven things. But we don't need all that." Again he gripped his mother, and stared down, not daring to look back at the corpse. I stood there in silence, thinking about the T-shirts that I'd seen in Tokyo proclaiming something like this idea: "Death is not an end but also a beginning". Just recently, a girl had passed me in the street wearing one. The slogan was printed on the back, while across her breasts she sported the single word: "Death".

"So!" he said with contrived decisiveness, "I call Yuki and some friends. Please make yourself at home."

At home! Only Masamichi on stoical autopilot could say such a thing in a decrepit hospital room with a dead father cooling on the bed and a grieving mother clutching his arm.

"Now we must meet many people," his mother said to me, searching hard for the English words. "Old friends, much family, long-time colleagues. So many!" And she traced a wide semicircle in the air with both hands. "In Japan, everybody come visit when dead. Only time when visit without inviting! Just arrive. That's it!" And she tried to smile, but crumpled back into that beseeching look. "I don't know how to say," she added despairingly.

I took the pointed way in which she was venting her frustration at having to receive all these people as a hint that now was the correct time for me to go. Her tenderly considerate tone suggested that she wanted to spare me the burden of witnessing her suffering.

As I left the hospital, overwhelmingly moved by the noble stoicism of this family, I wondered if it really mattered whether the "cheerfulness" which the Japanese insist on is sincere or not — in other words, whether their outer behaviour expresses a genuine inner mood. The fact is that most moods can be trained. Many can be pretended into existence. In this way, inner feelings can, with practice, come to resemble outer behaviour. So the claim to be "cheerful" could be self-validating. And the famous distinction between *honne* and *tatemae*, between one's personal feelings and one's socially expected appearance, which many Western observers see as *the* key to Japanese psychology, might not be so clear-cut after all. *Honne* is inevitably forged by *tatemae*, and the borders between the two are highly permeable.

For Westerners, sincerity is about expressing what you feel. For the Japanese, sincerity might be about feeling what you express, which is actually just another way of arriving at sincerity. For sincerity is, quite simply, the alignment of inner feeling and outer behaviour. Which of these two — inner feeling and outer behaviour — is the chicken and which the egg is a moot point.

18

Out on My Ear

"You must meet new lovely friend Tara," Yuki said suggestively as we had dinner one evening. "Masamichi meet her at architecture conference. She very smart young architect."

I suspected at once that Yuki's seal of approval didn't mean that Masamichi hadn't been there first. This was probably going to be a case of sloppy seconds. And yet, Tara... I felt there was something compactly poetic about that name. I found myself being besieged by images of a lithe woman, with long flowing black hair, a cute smile, silky-smooth legs, delightful little digits for fingers, a pert professional manner, intelligent, sparkling eyes and a fascinatingly self-absorbed face – a beauty, who was longing to meet me.

"When and where?" I was soon demanding of Yuki.

"Pick her up at my house next Tuesday at 9.00 p.m. Brind date!"

I spent half of the week quietly looking forward to my assignation, and on the day I arrived on the dot, something I rarely achieve. There were three people sitting in Yuki's living room, munching on snacks and toasting each other with white wine. A beautiful apparition answering to almost

137

all my preconceptions smiled up at me. Unfortunately, she was sitting next to a hunk in a tight T-shirt. Colossal biceps emerged from its short sleeves. On his other side sat another girl. She was wrapped in what can only be described as a three-man tent, made of taffeta. She was enormous. She was Tara.

I was about to join the threesome on the sofa, but Yuki was intent on ushering us out of the house at once. It would have been easier if she had allowed us a few minutes to get acquainted in her reassuring presence, but she obviously felt that she'd done her bit by introducing us. "Easier with four!" she whispered to me as the others put on their shoes. "By the way, her real name is Taeko, but when she did architecture Master's in America, she call herself Tara. It's her Western name."

The beginning of my date felt like an abduction. The hunk bundled me and Tara into the back of his car and we sped off towards her apartment — a luxurious penthouse in an expensive district of Tokyo. Tara settled back in the seat and hooked her arm around the handle of a wicker basket. Inside it, a felt toy dog was nestling in some sumptuous yellow fabric. She stroked the dog tenderly and whispered to it in sweet baby tones, looking around at me with seductively sad eyes. The hunk drove fast. I mumbled something about having made a reservation at one of my favourite sushi restaurants where the sea bream was especially fresh, and promised that I had earned the clout there to change the booking to four people at the last minute.

"Sushi for pensioners!" the hunk exclaimed from the front, and they all fell about guffawing.

"Plenty for you to eat at home," Tara promised me, running her fingers up the toy dog's long strands of fur, squeezing my arm, then bending over to rub her nose against the dog's.

Within fifteen minutes we were standing on the balcony of Tara's flat in a pleasant breeze, looking out over lattices of roads along which processions of cars meandered like glow-worms in the late-evening traffic. Tara opened a bottle of champagne, poured us all a glass – and professed to have just discovered that there was no food at all in the apartment.

"I don't know about you three…" I started.

"We don't want to go out, do we?" she broke in, in her rather energetic Japanese-American accent. "We'll just have to make do with champagne and whiskey."

The others enthusiastically agreed that they couldn't eat a thing. I gulped. I was starving.

"Eating no fun," said the hunk's girl.

"Other things fun," the hunk agreed.

Tara led us into her bedroom, a stainless-steel-and-glass boudoir with soft white lighting, designed by a friend of hers. The walls were draped with dark tapestries, between which hung several works of Araki Nobuyoshi, perhaps Japan's best known photographer. Most of them were shots of bored-looking nude women offering up their various apertures for scrutiny; some of the women were pregnant, others were tied up or otherwise in bondage, and one girl reclining nonchalantly was receiving cunnilingus from a lizard.

"I am in mourning for Leontine," Tara breathed to me in a flirtatiously plaintive way.

"Leontine?"

'My little poochie-pooch-poo," she explained, pouting irritatingly and speaking in a soft cooing voice. "She is now in Doggy Heaven with the Doggy Goddy. She was my baby, my everything. Now I only have *her* to remind me of Leontine." And she pointed at the basket with the toy dog that she had been stroking and cuddling in the car.

"You can't cry for ever," giggled the hunk's girlfriend, who had obviously lost interest in stories about Leontine's passing and ascension to Doggy Heaven. The hunk didn't care about Tara's poochie-pooch-poo either. He was engrossed in looking at a photo of two girls casually entwined in a lesbian embrace.

"Let's make ourselves comfortable," Tara threatened.

"Comfortable?" I said. I knew this spelt trouble.

"Why not get into bed?"

I stood awkwardly at the side of the large metal-framed bed as the three of them clambered in.

"Come on, it's alright," Tara teased me. "Just get in! Nothing to drink for you if you don't get in, you naughty naughty!"

So I slunk in, with the enthusiasm of a cat going for a swim in the canal, wondering what my alternative was. I could hardly sit on the end of the bed like a doctor performing his ward rounds. Nor did I want to leave. I wasn't sure what I wanted, though some take-out sushi would have been nice.

As Tara snuggled up to me, I pretended to myself that I was performing a stint of social services in a very expensively appointed clinic, or else that this was all part of my getting to know the Japanese.

"All those aspects of Japan that I have carefully sought out," I reprimanded myself silently, "all those so-called 'experiences' I have had: they've actually been highly controlled, highly unthreatening." This thought alone compelled me to stay, to be daring, to challenge myself – though I would have much preferred to make my excuses and leave this deeply unwished-for encounter with a trio of well-organized, self-confident and autonomous young Japanese professionals. I laughed inwardly at memories of starchy Noh plays, tea ceremonies performed by women with permafrost expressions, and male Kabuki actors playing damsels in distress with that sing-song shriek that is supposed to depict a woman taken aback by sudden grief.

Tara turned to face me, as the other two cuddled and confided and laughed in whispers. I feared the worst.

I got it. As she puckered up her lips and moved in for the kill, I was assailed by a burst of insupportably bad, absolutely rancid breath.

I jerked back and started asking her urgently about contemporary Japanese architects. What were they doing? Where were they going? Were there different schools? Trends? Why were they more successful abroad than in Japan itself? Did Masamichi's work interest her? I clasped her shoulders in a vice-like grip to hold her off, making no pretence about rebuffing her. The whiskey bottle stood half-empty on the little glass-and-metal designer table next to the bed.

"Masamichi is a fake," she averred. "That's not real architecture. He designs standard offices and homes. Uninteresting stuff!" Again she lurched at me and tried to press her mouth to mine, exhaling another blast of poisonous breath into my face. I turned away.

"You don't find me attractive because I am fat," she snarled at me while stroking my neck. "I know that's the reason. Men used to desire me madly."

"You are attractive, most attractive," I muttered, seizing the opportunity for dialogue and hoping that it might stem her erotic fury. "I just hardly know you."

"Well then, what's wrong with me?" she enquired, gently placing her other hand on my chest. She started undoing my shirt buttons.

Though I was revolted, I couldn't help admiring her shameless self-possession, even as she was leading the charge in a rape scene. The surroundings, too, seemed so composed, so organized, so impressive. They somehow justified the instant, Dionysiac adventures she was hankering after. I just wished she could be a little more reserved while in bed with a reluctant stranger, or perhaps introduce a preliminary stage into her seduction ritual. Such as brushing her teeth.

"Well?" she exclaimed impatiently – and she ripped off her blouse and straddled me. Two enormous breasts sprang out and quivered before my now horrified eyes. The hunk and his girl were already getting it on next to us. Reassuring images of a more peaceful evening – perhaps enjoying seconds of sea-urchin sashimi, or participating in the serenity of an incense ceremony – flashed involuntarily through my mind. Even the grimy philosophy department at Todai made a fleeting appearance, the first time that its dilapidated and forlorn rooms had managed to comfort me.

"No, I'm not on for it," I insisted. "I'm definitely not."

"Yes you are!" she countered. She was drunk and lusty. I realized that manoeuvring her off me would be a logistical challenge of considerable proportions. As I pondered my options, she grabbed my shirt with one hand and tried to tear it off, while the other hand reached down to unbutton my trousers. I seized her plump arms and tugged her to the right, then to the left, then to the right again, in a futile effort to get her off me. She bent down and again planted her gas-attack mouth on mine. I pushed her aggressively away – my resolve stiffened by that further encounter with her halitosis. Then she bit my ear, viciously.

"Get the hell off…" I yelled, as my ear reeled from its first experience of cannibalism.

As I finally wrestled free of her, the white pillow under my head fell to the floor, now stained with a large patch of blood. The other two had emerged from their writhings to observe the fun. I leapt out of bed, the three of them laughing out loud at me as I silently located my jacket and coat. Their expressions said: "Why chicken out now? Not much has happened yet anyway." Araki's photographs echoed this message, even amplified it. Anything seemed unadventurous compared to what his girls might get up to. I felt defiant and also oddly sheepish. But I had one overriding aim: to make it to the front door without either Tara's breath or her anger getting the better of me.

The dark streets outside felt like a golden oasis of liberty. As I walked to the local railway station, I could have hugged every passer-by, every drunken salaryman, for showing enough respect to ignore me. Every now and then I was sure that someone would pounce from out of a dark alley, but people seemed to be going out of their way not to touch me.

I called Yuki from the deserted station after being told that I had missed the last train back to Kamakura. I gave her an earful then and there. She immediately invited me to stay the night. When I got to her house, she was sympathetic – although not wholly mortified.

"But Masamichi said Tara so nice and so competent," she said. "Perfect for you. I think intelligent more important for you than good-looking."

"Intelligent?" I gasped. "She's mad!"

"But she seem so good person to us," Yuki kept saying, on autopilot. "Maybe you overreacting."

"She tried to bite my ear off!"

"Excellent professional reputation," Yuki observed.

"She bit half my ear off!"

"She very nice to animals," Yuki countered.

"Yes, nicer than to humans."

"Pity you don't like. I thought she so perfect for you."

I gave up resisting. It was clear that Yuki didn't want to know, and anyway there's no arguing with a Japanese non-sequitur stubbornly maintained. All I could do was stagger off to bed, nursing my stinging ear, and worry about how many infectious diseases Tara's furred teeth had landed me with. I lay awake for half the night, the whole grotesque scene replaying in my mind on an endless loop, hoping that Leontine in Doggy Heaven with the Doggy Goddy was watching over my ear and restraining the advances of her mistress's bacteria. Leontine, I was sure, had made the right decision to leave her mistress for a better world. She was a smart dog.

19

Pure Blood

A fortnight had passed since Mr and Mrs Yamazaki's daughter Akiko had returned from her wedding in Florida, and her enthusiasm was still as fresh as her ruddy country face.

"Disneyland is Paradise!"

These were almost the only English words she could say, but say them she did, over and over again, every time another memory leapt into her mind: the "cute" minister who had donned a Mickey Mouse uniform after the ceremony; the wedding carriage drawn by four golden steeds; the frolic with Minnie Mouse at the reception; the red velvet Scarlett O'Hara dress she had been given to wear at the ball.

"What about saying 'I do'?" I asked her. "Surely you need to know those two words to get married in Disneyland?" But all such practical problems had been taken care of by the Tokyo travel agency: a Japanese minister had been flown over to conduct the ceremony, and seven newly married Japanese couples had taken the same honeymoon together, accompanied by a guide and interpreter. No need for English had arisen.

For the next year, or at least until either she or her husband got a good job, Akiko would have to live with her parents up in the Nagano Alps, about ninety minutes north of Tokyo by bullet train. The house was a small wooden bungalow with a long living room, a couple of bedrooms, a tiny kitchen, and a traditional bathroom. An inside toilet had recently been added, but it was freezing cold, even in March. My urine steamed in the chilly air like piping-hot miso soup, and when the flusher failed to work at night I knew that the water in the tank had frozen solid.

The Yamazakis were in their late fifties. They owned a kimono-weaving business that had been in the family for four generations, specializing in the luxury end of the market. Five months were required to make enough fine linen material – or *echigo jofu* – for one kimono. Walking round the small workshop next to their house, you could see why; the threads, as thin as hairs, were prepared entirely by hand, and the kimono linen was woven on an ancient machine. There were six employees engaged in this painstaking labour, half of them tiny hunchbacked old ladies who had been working there all their lives.

One of them struck my attention immediately. She was seventy-two and less than five feet tall, with a tangle of white hair done up into a bun, and deep-set eyes glowing impishly out of her shrivelled face. For hours on end she sat on the floor, bent intently over spools of thread that she meticulously starched – strand by strand – stopping only to cut off tiny snags with a minute pair of scissors. Her absolute stillness and focus made me feel distinctly twitchy. Nothing had changed here for years, although in most other respects the Yamazakis were a thoroughly modern family.

Mitsuo and Ikuko Yamazaki had invited me to visit them at Yuki's suggestion. "This is rural Japan," Yuki had warned me. "Please arrive as Santa Claus with many gifts. Can be cheap, but must be plenty."

It was valuable advice. My visit to this traditional family was marked by a continuous process of giving on both sides. On arrival I was presented with a bottle of local sake. Within another hour or two, the sake had been followed by a couple of furry mascots resembling mountain animals. Soon after came a box of sweet-bean cakes, and then a tiny porcelain bowl decorated with painted wild flowers. A constant stream of cooked delicacies also appeared. The slightest pause in conversation would trigger the arrival of another delicious surprise, hastily fetched by Mrs Yamazaki from the kitchen.

With almost equal frequency, I felt obliged to get up and hand out my own offerings – as nonchalantly and spontaneously as they handed me theirs. Though everybody knew that the gifts were strictly reciprocal, they were not to appear that way. Visits to or from neighbours involved the same procedure. A present had to be conveniently to hand.

The first neighbour to look in, perhaps to inspect this rare appearance of a *gaigin* in town, was "Uncle", the village headman. His role was to resolve disputes, manage village-owned property, sign contracts for public works, supervise the recording of births, marriages and deaths, and coordinate representations by the community to the local city government. His most important duty was to ensure that the village's annual budget always got spent – preferably on useful things, but if that wasn't possible, then useless ones would do – otherwise there'd be a lower grant in future from the City and Prefectural authorities. Slow in speech, quick in wit, red-faced from a decades-old enthusiasm for sake, Uncle was a down-to-earth man whose presence commanded respect. He started quizzing me as soon as he arrived.

He was as direct as they come, which in Japan can be very direct indeed. The way he guffawed at some of my answers – to questions as banal as when I arrived in Nagano, who my girlfriend was, and whether I drank green tea – was unsettling. I never quite figured out what this kind of laughter meant in Japan, but it was seldom triggered by anything funny. It felt like a smokescreen for uncertainty about how to evaluate a foreigner; perhaps it was also camouflaging a sense of superiority or inferiority, or both. The point that really had him in stitches, however, was the fact that I was a philosopher. His reaction was similar to that of the gardener in Kyoto.

"Are you a monk?" he asked sardonically after he'd stopped laughing. "You wander about with a begging bowl and a big wicker hat and straw sandals?"

"No. Even in Japan not all philosophers are monks."

"So why are you a philosopher? You don't like women? Philosophy means escaping from worry and women and war – the normal conditions of life! I might even envy you!"

I evaded his put-down by mumbling something about the impossibility of justifying any life choice. He seemed nonplussed by this answer, so I decided to tease him with a true reason for doing philosophy:

"There's another abnormal condition that draws people to philosophy: the inability or refusal to have a home in one place. Philosophy is the search for many homes. Perhaps," I ventured, "the Japanese are too securely at home to be philosophers."

"We Japanese are not philosophers," he conceded proudly. "We have our philosophy, of course; but we prefer not to speak about it."

I agreed with this wholeheartedly: "You don't need to spell out your philosophy unless your roots are endangered, unless the question of your identity becomes a conscious, live problem."

"Like the Jews," he said, without a trace of anti-Semitism.

"Yes. In the West we are all becoming Jews," I replied, tongue-in-cheek.

"You are right, May-san. We Japanese do not need philosophy. We are still racially pure. Perhaps we are the last racially pure people."

I found this a shocking gloss on my point, and yet the way he said it was too "innocent" to be sinister. Japan must be the only nation in the world where a *blut-und-boden* – blood-and-soil – mythology is openly voiced in an inoffensive, even naive, way. People don't seem to associate it with Nazi evil, or with names like Auschwitz.

"But if we are forced to accept more foreign influence, then we will need more philosophy," he persisted, warming to the theme. "Foreigners will endanger our identity. Then we will import their philosophy in order to regain the identity they destroyed." He grinned with satisfaction as he drew his conclusion: "Foreigners will try to cure the disease they cause us. But the cure will simply lead to further disease."

Only in Japan could such opinions sound benign. But the instincts they expressed hadn't sprung up just now. They had been imbibed with his mother's milk.

"So how do you do philosophy here in Japan?" he asked me.

"I work at Tokyo University," I answered, slightly sheepishly, given how much I had been teased about the place.

"Tokyo University," he whispered, incredulous. His hitherto mobile face took on an aspect of stunned admiration.

Mr and Mrs Yamazaki, who had been impassive while
we talked about philosophy, stared at me as if I were a god
freshly arrived from the heavens. A reverent silence fell
over the room. Then Mrs Yamazaki, her eyes dilating in
submission, stammered: "We never thought we would have
a professor from Tokyo University in our house. This is a
great honour. We couldn't even aspire to study there, let
alone to be a professor."

She looked humbly at her daughter. "Could you ever
imagine going to Todai, Akiko-chan?"

"I never thought about it," Akiko answered, shrugging
her shoulders. "Who cares about Todai, for God's sake?" was
her real expression. "What's it got to do with anything?" She
was lounging on the floor, lazily stroking the furry tummy
of a teddy bear. It certainly seemed well-travelled: clipped
to its open fur coat were souvenirs of the Eiffel Tower, the
Statue of Liberty, the Beefeaters at the Tower of London
and other evidence of globe-trotting. And around its neck
was a tag containing pictures of happy families of teddy
bears sitting in Pullman restaurant cars, watching vintage
aircraft displays, dressed up as desert sheikhs posing before a
toy mosque, taking English High Tea, hiking in the alps, and
living in igloos. Over the pictures there was a caption that
read: "Happiness is a cute collection of cuddly teddy bears
who love to make people smile."

"Such heights are completely beyond our hopes,"
Mrs Yamazaki continued, ignoring her daughter's apathy.
"*Completely.*" Then, to her husband, "Mitsuo-san, I never
thought this would happen to us! We're under one roof
with a Todai professor! In *this* room! I have shaken hands
and shared food with a Todai professor!"

This was turning into theatre of the absurd.

"Isn't it true that students at Todai are not allowed to

walk in their professor's shadow?" Mrs Yamazaki asked in a girly voice that grated with her years, as I tried not to snigger at the image she had just conjured up.

It's certainly true that there is an old Japanese saying along those lines – *Sanjaku satte shino kagewo fumazu*, or "Teachers are so venerable that it is impertinent for students to approach close enough to step on their shadows" – but I suspected that students had been stepping across professors' shadows with impunity for decades. "On sunny winter afternoons like this, when the shadows are long," Mrs Yamazaki continued, poetically, "your students must follow far behind you!" And she looked at me all coy and starstruck.

"Er, that is most definitely not the case," I replied, thinking of my slack-jawed students slouching comatose over their desks, occasionally stirring to answer a mobile phone. "Most of my students pity me for not having a more lucrative job."

"Can philosophy help with understanding death?" Uncle put in unexpectedly, from left field, in a flat and slightly resentful voice, as if unwilling to accept my self-deprecation. Awe had drained his expression of colour.

"That's probably what it's least good for," I answered. "Philosophers, like the Epicureans and Stoics, have talked a lot about death, but most of us don't fear death, we fear dying: the incomprehensible and often dreadfully painful moment of transition when we go from being something to being nothing."

"What about facing the death of a loved one, rather than one's own death?" Uncle continued, in a curious tone, as though something were on his mind. "Sometimes I wonder," he mused, working his way towards his main point, "how one deals with the death of someone…"

But his voice petered out.

"Someone?"

"Well, someone whom one once loved – but now despises. Someone who has betrayed his group."

"I see."

"Someone," Uncle finished, his eyes dark and forbidding, "who has caused his whole society to lose face."

"This must be dreadful," I ventured, feeling my way in cautiously. "You don't even know whether you want to mourn. It's tormenting – and probably impossible – to take leave of people you loved without being able to mourn them or somehow to appreciate them."

The story came out, in sudden rushes and reluctant concessions. One of the village's most accomplished sons had died suddenly in a car accident, just a couple of days previously. He was a brilliant lawyer, in his mid-thirties, destined, as everyone saw it, to become a district magistrate or something even higher. As he was driving home in freezing fog from a hearing in a neighbouring town, he had collided head-on with a lorry and had been killed outright. The calamity had bereaved at least a dozen people in the village to whom he was related. And it had deprived its inhabitants of their most articulate advocate in the local City Assembly. No one in the village had been better at understanding the machinations of politicians and bureaucrats. His death would mean fewer roads and public works for the village and its environs, and fewer subsidies all round.

The subtext of Uncle's lament was that all this would make his own life a lot harder, not only because he would have more work to do himself, but because his standing would be damaged. It was obvious that although he was good at village politics – keeping on cordial terms with people, resolving minor disagreements, chairing the village assembly, maintaining careful records – he was out of his depth when it came to dealing with the more complex City and prefectural bureaucracies. He had relied on the dead man to do all that.

It gradually emerged, though, that by far his greatest concern was that a planned museum for arts and crafts might be shelved. He nervously fished from his pocket an artist's impression of the projected structure, which showed a huge wooden building, in the style of a Swiss chalet, with granite floors, pillars of the finest pine wood, a magnificent spiral staircase with a glass and stainless-steel banister, and large windows set in gleaming aluminium frames. As to the likely contents of this impressive edifice, he was distinctly coy. In terms of "culture", the village didn't seem to have much to show for itself beyond a few weaving machines, "traditional peasant sandals", articles of "mountain clothing" and some kitschy oil paintings. It was impossible to resist the thought that he had more in mind than preserving the village's artistic riches or sustaining the pride of its inhabitants. The kickbacks on a building as lavish as this would certainly finance a lot more than a new kitchen for his wife or an upgraded SUV.

As I learnt more and more about the situation, Mr and Mrs Yamazaki occasionally chipped in. They had known the ambitious and resourceful young man all his life. Mrs Yamazaki wept restrained tears for his widowed mother, who had to face this tragedy alone in her old age. Mr Yamazaki went over to the Shinto family altar at the other end of the long living room and stood before it in glum contemplation.

"Is there a widow?" I asked. "Any children?"

Stony silence. Everyone looked down. Then Uncle replied curtly:

"No. None."

Excruciating tension crackled in his reply, and we all fell silent. The atmosphere in the room was dark enough to warrant the blackest speculations about the dead man's disgrace – theft, fraud, murder – but pretty soon I guessed that this illustrious village prodigy had been guilty of nothing more than being gay.

Worse still, he had refused the tacit condition for being gay in Japan, except at the bohemian fringes of society: taking a wife. Here in the countryside this condition was probably imposed even more strictly than in the cities and big corporations. Though Japan once had a long tradition of cultivating homoeroticism as an ideal form of love, this was always the preserve of the warrior classes. Youthful male beauty might have been all the rage among the samurai, as it had been in ancient Greece, but down on the farm such cults had no place.

An unspoken consensus closed the subject with the arrival of a great Japanese dinner, flush with the most exquisite colours, textures and smells. The dishes were paraded in: fiddlehead ferns sautéed in sesame oil and seasoned with a soy-flavoured broth; daikon radish and carrots finely sliced into hair-like threads, kneaded with salt, rinsed, then marinated in a sweet-vinegar dressing; the easily mispronounced *fukinotoo* – bitter flower buds of the butterbur, parboiled, sautéed in sesame oil, and mixed with a miso and sake dressing; a suite of small dishes with super-fresh simmered vegetables, taro potatoes, dried and reconstituted wheat gluten wheels, octopus, deep-fried fish cakes, tofu of various kinds, and new akebia leaf buds; and, of course, home-grown glutinous rice.

For now, Uncle's tortured musings were silenced.

20

THE MYSTERIOUS HOT-WATER BOTTLE

As we criss-crossed our chopsticks over these delicacies, impatiently sampling new ones, then returning lustily to those whose ravishing attack we craved yet again, the atmosphere steadily lightened. My sake glass, whose tiny size could deceive the most careful drinker that he was imbibing modestly, was refilled more times than I could count with locally brewed sakes. And while we gorged, Mr Yamazaki regaled us in painstaking detail with how he had hand-gathered the ingredients we were eating, mostly from the surrounding mountains. The fiddlehead ferns had to be found in the early and still snowy spring, dried on a mat in the sun, kneaded, dried again, and reconstituted before use. The akebia leaf buds also had to be picked in the mountains in the early spring. Some of the mushrooms we were eating could be found only on east-facing slopes, others only on a particular species of oak tree, yet more only in the pine forest. There was the *enokitake*, found on the *enoki* tree, the *myoga*, which heralded Spring, and a list as long as your arm of other types, some preserved, but most freshly picked.

Beneath the low square table, our outstretched legs were kept blissfully warm by the *kotatsu*, a coiled heating element surrounded by an insulating quilted skirt at which Japanese families and their friends gather in winter. The intimacy of a *kotatsu* is magical: everyone's legs are huddled under the table, and the gentle heat is so even that it seems to flow into you from other people rather than from a filament. This hidden closeness – your legs are concealed by the table and its broad skirting, while the rest of you retains its privacy and, more or less, its coldness – is somehow very Japanese in its discreet intensity. And it affords a unique sense of cosy unity among those present, quite different from, say, a fireplace, where the heat emanates from a single source that is both more violent and more distant. No wonder the *kotatsu* is the traditional centre of a Japanese home, a place where the many formalities and strains of society can be abandoned, if only under the table.

All the while, there had actually been another person present, but she hardly said or heard anything. Grandmother Yamazaki, Mitsuo's mother, lived in the house but normally appeared only for meals. She was a truculent soul, and as tough as old leather. Though she was too deaf, and probably also too pig-headed, to join in with the conversation, she would break her silence every so often to interject an abrupt comment, complaint, command, or all three. She sat there sourly, grumpily accepting as her due Ikuko's spectacular dishes, whose beautiful presentation she ruined by turning over the food with her chopsticks to check that it passed muster. If satisfied, she would eat with picky caution, as if the cook were on probation. If not satisfied, she rudely pushed aside her plate for Ikuko to clear away. I didn't hear a word of appreciation from her.

Something must have happened that night to make Ikuko lose her patience. So controlled was her rage at Grandmother Yamazaki that I didn't realize anything was amiss until the old woman summarily stood up and left the room, leaving a viscous silence in her wake. At first I thought she was just going to bed. Then I understood that she had deeply offended them by disparaging – of all things – Ikuko's hospitality. Here I was, she said, a Todai professor and a foreigner, and Ikuko had given me things like raw fish, tofu and sake that a Westerner couldn't possibly be expected to like, let alone digest. How anyone could be so thoughtless was entirely beyond her – she herself would never have done this to me; her daughter-in-law was ruining the good Yamazaki name, and not for the first time.

This was a burden too much for Ikuko. Grandmother's venom, the news of the death, the day-long labour of preparing our dinner, Uncle's endless visit, and the excitement of hosting a minor god from Todai, had all left her exhausted. With her mother-in-law gone, the last dish served, and uncounted sake bottles drained, her poise imploded. Ignored by her menfolk, she slumped lower and lower onto the floor, vanishing altogether under the *kotatsu* – except for her head with its tousled half-undone bun – and finally fell asleep.

Mitsuo was visibly relieved at the departure of all his women – his daughter Akiko had retired earlier to leaf through a catalogue of sports cars, hoping to find one she could afford with her wedding money – and he seized the moment to abandon the ruins of our dinner and the equally stale atmosphere left by the evening's conversation. He sealed off the dining area with a Chinese screen, and sat Uncle and me down at the *irori*, a warming hearth with a kettle on it – which, like the *kotatsu*, is another of those wonderful inducements to relaxed proximity in this country of polite distance. Slowly and expertly, he prepared green tea, not by brewing it with hot water, but by pressing crushed ice hard onto dried tea leaves in a beautiful little

Chinese teapot, a technique he had picked up in Kyoto. This arduous procedure produced tiny quantities of dense green liquid, which looked and tasted like the absolute essence of Japanese tea. It was pure nectar: fresh, intense, three-dimensional, refined. Like great wine, the smallest drop attacked your palate with its raw power, then spread out to all sides of your mouth, releasing a cascade of flavours on its way, to reveal finally its full depth and subtlety as it tailed off to a glorious finish.

While I lingered over the tea, trying to discipline myself to a drop at a time, Mitsuo and Uncle settled down to discuss the arrangements for next weekend's so-called "Naked Festival", or *hadaka matsuri*, at a nearby Shinto shrine. In an outpouring of Dionysiac flamboyance, drunken young men, wearing nothing but flimsy loincloths, run wildly across the snow carrying enormous candles – one metre high and half a metre across – spraying their white molten wax into the predominantly female crowd, before jumping headlong into freezing water. Though few today know much about the rites of purification which are the purpose of this ancient religious festival, the symbolism seems evident, and the opportunity to exhibit one's physique, stamina and raw passion is relished by participants and spectators alike.

"He would have been too old," Uncle was saying, the death of the gay lawyer still on his mind.

"Yes, but he still wanted to do it. He was very fit. Amazing body for his age," Mitsuo countered.

"Admit it: it was getting embarrassing," said Uncle. "His preoccupation with his body. At that age. Tanning it under lamps. Exercising with all those machines. Mad. But he was not the kind of person you could stop. Real samurai spirit: obsessed with physical and mental endurance. You've got to admire it. He had will."

"Does everybody on the organizing committee know?"

"Yes, I've told them all."

"So why was I the last to hear about it?" Mitsuo asked peevishly.

"You were all celebrating Akiko's wedding and their return from Florida. So I wasn't going to upset your happiness until I had to. By the way, the funeral is tomorrow morning at 9 a.m."

Tomorrow at nine! And now it was 2 a.m. It was time for sleep, and especially for a break from the strain of being an outsider in this house. It was clear that Mitsuo and Uncle weren't at all tired, and that they were going to keep chatting and drinking for a long time yet. The only problem was that my futon was within spitting distance of the *irori* where they were still sitting, and my ability to sleep surrounded by light, noise and smoke in a strange room was just not up to the Japanese standard. But it was either that or no sleep at all; so when Mitsuo went to fetch some whiskey, I sloped off to the bathroom to prepare for bed.

In the dark, cold corridor, I lost my way and only discovered I was in the kitchen when a pile of crockery crashed to the ground and broke into a hundred pieces. Intensely embarrassed, I fumbled about in vain for a light and a moment later found myself inadvertently stroking Mitsuo's arm as he came to rescue me. As the rubble was illuminated, my embarrassment turned to horror. I had broken five or six ceramic dishes, a couple of sake glasses and a teacup, all of them heirlooms that had been brought out in my honour.

Mitsuo's kindness was overwhelming. "No problem, no problem," he kept repeating as he kicked aside the largest fragments. "We can easily replace them" – which was almost certainly untrue. "Please enjoy your bath." And without a hint of artifice, he dismissed the whole mess with a wave of his arm and led me to the bathroom.

"Please get undressed," he said, waiting for me to hand him my clothes.

"No, no, it's OK," I said, not in the mood for the open-mouthed gawping that goes on in public baths when *gaigin* disrobe.

"*Dozo*," he said, standing stock-still, awaiting my nudity.

"What the hell!" I thought to myself, and stripped to the bone, handing him my clothes, which he folded into a neat pile and placed in a little basket. He tactfully resisted staring at my hairy chest and legs, or checking whether the legendary endowment of the Western male actually matched the reality.

"*Dozo*," he repeated, pointing to the full tub of water, with its floating patches of oily scum and particulate matter, which most of the family had already enjoyed. Now, however, I procrastinated. Sharing everyone's water, Japanese-style, in a bathroom just above freezing point was not my idea of a soothing soak. So I thanked him for his kindness, took a quick shower, and gave the tub a wide berth. Then I stole back into the living room, fetched my hot-water bottle – my one defence against freezing Japanese bedrooms – and was just about to go searching for a kettle when I heard the two men falling about themselves with hilarity. I looked round startled.

They were pointing at me, laughing helplessly.

"What's the matter?" I asked, racing to tune in to their merriment. No answer; they were laughing too hard. Could it be my striped pyjamas? Or was it the sight of me wearing a Japanese cotton dressing gown, a *yukata*, over my pyjamas? – a combination which in Japan seems to convey all the dignity of going to bed in Wellington boots and a tutu. Or maybe it was my ungainly webbed toes that had set them off? – a sore point at the best of times, but especially in this country of foot fetishists.

No, it was my hot-water bottle. As they motioned to inspect this strange contraption, mirth turned to amazement, as if a UFO had landed in their midst. Flipping it over and over, no detail was too banal to merit comment: the serrated rubber; the little flap at the base; the white screw top; the woolly cover. You could imagine Mitsuo's workshop switching its product range and perfecting the hot-water bottle beyond anything hitherto conceived by the West. The astonished curiosity with which they inspected it, the speed with which they grasped its construction and came up with improvements, amazed me. There is a whole aesthetic in the way Japanese relate to the objects of their attention, whether they are preparing food, weaving kimonos, sweeping the streets, making cameras, or sawing wood. The way their hands touch the object, the way their eyes fix on it, betrays a sensibility of the rarest kind: direct, precise, immediate, and in true relationship to whatever it engages. Their approach to the mechanical is always spirited, always charged with passion, never drab or "alienated" in the way that it can be in the West, at least outside the Germanic countries.

"Just a moment, please," Mitsuo said excitedly as he ran out of the room, returning some seconds later with an oval, flat object, like a large stingray or Dover sole made of corrugated iron – the Japanese hot-water bottle. He slipped on his reading glasses, then compared the two artefacts under the light with fierce concentration. "Why does yours have such rounded edges, when you need maximum surface area to warm yourself?" he asked, looking at me over his glasses as if I were a lifelong expert on the matter, albeit one who had lost his touch. "Why is it made of rubber, when metal conducts heat so much more efficiently? How strange that you don't use a clip to keep in the water like we do!" And he tested his clip against my screw top as if he were seeking the philosopher's stone.

I was used to this sort of bemused hilarity at *gaigin* and all their works, but that it could extend to the intricacies of a hot-water bottle was a new one on me. Mercifully, it was dawning on Uncle, ever conscious of his status, that examining this primitive device for longer than was needed to poke fun at it was beneath his dignity, and he presently persuaded the obsessed Mitsuo to return it to me and join him back at the *irori*.

The two men went on talking about plans for the festival of nakedness, the finances of the village, the problem of dwindling government subsidies, the consequence of an awkward death, and probably a lot more besides. But I must have become a little more Japanese in my habits because, amid all the burble and the banter, I gradually fell asleep.

21

Four Gangsters and a Funeral

The next morning I was awakened by a shuffling sound. It was Mitsuo coming in to pay his daily homage to the family shrine, which was near my futon in a corner of the living room. I pretended to be asleep while watching him meditate before a little Buddha surrounded by fruit, flowers, incense, miniature ancestral gravestones and pictures of recently deceased relatives, the largest and newest being his father, who Ikuko told me had died only the previous year.

After my freezing ablutions, I joined the others by the *kotatsu* for breakfast. Again the table was blanketed with delicacies: grilled salted salmon, grilled mackerel complete with skin and head, steamed mountain vegetables, home-cured pickles, small pieces of sweet omelette resting on a bamboo leaf, fluffy white rice and miso soup. But the real challenge was a side-dish called *natto*: fermented soya beans with a sticky, stringy texture and a faint whiff of ammonia. The Japanese regard *natto* as the absolute litmus test of whether a foreigner can handle their food. Even locals can have a tough time with it. Masamichi, for example, once told me that this gooey glutinous mass with its pungent smell was fit only for pigs; but in small doses and if sufficiently fresh it can be delicious, especially when combined with blander things like boiled vegetables and rice. It certainly jolted me into wakefulness much more effectively than cornflakes or toast.

Though it was only 8.30 on a Sunday morning, Ikuko and Mitsuo had already done a couple of hours in the workshop. They were smartly dressed in black, ready for the funeral. By 9.30, a bit late because of our long breakfast, we made it to the house of the deceased. It was a cold, sunny morning; the air was crisp and clean, and the crowd of villagers and relatives, at least eighty of them, wrapped in thick coats and hats, were gathered outside in silent respect. All the doors and sliding windows had been removed from the front of the house, which was festooned with garlands of flowers and white cloth crossed with broad black stripes. The main room had been turned into something like a shrine, complete with robed attendants and an altar on a tiered stand, underneath which rested the coffin surrounded by dozens of white chrysanthemums.

As we stood in the cold trying to hear what was happening inside, Mitsuo patted me on the arm and handed me a small envelope. "Please leave this for his mother," he said, with a look that said, "I'll explain everything afterwards." I peeked inside and saw two crisp 5,000-Yen notes. I was about to present $100 of someone else's money to a lady I had never met before: the gift-giving ritual, much honoured the previous afternoon, was clearly swinging into a higher gear. Though funerals were cheaper than weddings – where you might have to hand over upwards of $200, and much more at a really smart one – this still seemed a lot to be giving a perfect stranger in a remote mountain village.

We shuffled around on our feet for a good hour, trying to keep warm and straining to catch the virtually inaudible service. Snatches of chants and sermons, and perhaps a eulogy, seeped out intermittently from the living room. Otherwise the high banks of snow on either side of the road absorbed the little sound that emerged. Everyone, including small children, stood to attention like frozen sentries, mute with uncomprehending grief. The thick silence was oppressive, almost asphyxiating, and the vast cold landscape everywhere around us felt cruelly unresponsive and maddeningly still. It came as a relief when a bent old lady, eyes cast inconsolably downwards, emerged from the house and worked her way patiently through the crowd accepting whispered condolences and discreetly squeezing the hands of intimates. But it was an unforgettably wrenching moment when, pausing by me, she reciprocated my anonymous bow, her tiny figure rigid with sorrow, and I suddenly felt myself at the centre of a community overwhelmed by the brutality of its bereavement.

Then everyone removed their hats and bowed their heads still lower in respect and dismay. In the front room of the house the coffin was being prepared for a hearse that was backing up to receive it. This was a hearse with a difference: a black estate car minus its top, carrying an enormous, highly ornate, pyramidal shrine decorated with elaborately carved wood, garish paintings and a coronet of jingling bells.

The atmosphere of mourning quickly became charged with unease when the pall-bearers appeared out of nowhere to carry the coffin to the hearse. Four hoods strode onto the scene in dark glasses, golden earrings and sharp black suits, as if auditioning for a movie. All wore violently coloured shirts: leopard skin, crimson, yellow and gold, bright green and blue. At first, I thought the men must be some particularly snappy undertakers. Then Mitsuo, conveying

the general bafflement, whispered to me: "Must be his
friends! Strange situation, don't you think?" They looked
a bit like the bouncers who stood guard in black tuxedos
outside Roppongi's seedier nightspots, and they were
clearly not people to mess with. Tall, tough, tanned, their
latent aggression wasn't feigned, unlike that of the leather-
jacketed bike gangs who roam the streets in Japan. They
were operators, not poseurs: it was easy to imagine them as
loan sharks cruising in big black Mercedes, carrying flick
knives and brown envelopes stuffed with cash.

They pulled out of the car an accordion, a guitar and
two *shakuhachi* – the traditional Japanese wind instrument
that looks like a large recorder – and started to serenade
the dead man. This was nothing like the Last Post, nothing
solemn or even measured, but a galloping harmonic mess
for a group of instruments whose tonalities clashed at every
turn. Yet something about the loyalty, tenderness, clumsiness
of this gesture was strangely touching. The respects they
were paying were sincere and intensely felt.

At this point, it looked as if the four men were hijacking
the funeral. The priests were still in the living room, the
mother had melted into the mourners, and everyone was
somehow sealed off from the deceased by this Praetorian
Guard of – it was obvious to all now – his boyfriend and three
close associates. As the sense of separation became palpable,
an air of scandal descended. Whispers gave way to general
burble, as the implications became clear: the dead man had
not just represented the villagers in the neighbouring town,
but was mixed up there with a gay scene, and had links
to gangsterism. As wild speculations about his antics leapt
through the crowd, mourning surrendered to a sense of
betrayal. Almost before my eyes, I could feel a whole village,
attached to this son by years of familiarity and pride and

gratitude, turn abruptly away from him, and cast him into a terrible darkness of suspicion and condemnation. Nobody *did* anything, of course. But the spirit of rejection filled the air and made it thick with the violence of banishment.

And there, still consoled by her community, yet soon to be edged out of it as surely as the dead man himself, was the diminutive, broken old woman. The evidence of her son's secret life was probably entirely new to her, and she clearly couldn't take it in. She seemed more alone, more confused, more pitiful than ever.

Before the new attitude to the deceased could really impose itself, or the old attitude be abandoned, the hearse started moving towards us, crushing the freshly fallen snow as it made its stately progress. One felt that it ought to linger for a while, long enough for people to control their rising disgust, long enough to narrow the chasm that had so suddenly opened between the dead man and his community, long enough for a cold peace to be stitched up with the corpse before it vanished. A few intrepid souls split off from the crowd and followed the black-suited vanguard. The old mother, supported by some friends and relatives, followed up the rear of the cortège. After a short distance the hearse stopped again: the followers piled into a minibus and the two vehicles continued at a faster pace towards the crematorium – the place where practically everyone in this cramped country ends up.

As soon as the hearse had disappeared, we joined a queue to pay our respects at the altar in the living room, then deposited our gifts of money on a small table, where a pretty teenager, visibly struggling to retain her composure, stowed them safely in a metal box. On the altar were placed an incense burner, a bowl of rice, flowers, cakes and further monetary gifts of condolence.

By the time we re-emerged, the crowd had almost entirely dispersed, along with its intensely compacted series of moods, first of loss, then of shock, finally of repudiation. We walked back to the Yamazakis' home in silence. Somehow, this funeral had dealt them a crushing blow. Uncle joined us unexpectedly, together with his wife, whom he had so far kept well-hidden. You could feel his sense of helplessness, even of anger, that the old mores were no longer predictable or enforceable. And that the power of the locality – as strong in Japan as anywhere in the world – was being eroded before his eyes. Later on, he spoke of his fear of a vast, destructive and uncontrollable world in which the village was losing its identity and autonomy to the town, the town to the prefectural capital, the prefectural capital to Tokyo, Tokyo to the globe, and everywhere to cable and satellite and Internet. This small community in the remote Nagano Alps would never be the same again. Trust had been betrayed – trivially for a great city, drastically for this tiny village. A man who had honoured his people by day had dishonoured them by night. They had believed that he always returned to his mother and his community after a splendid day's work in the city. Perhaps he usually did. But in reality he had abandoned the village long before he died, and now he would never be coming home.

22

PROFESSOR X

Halfway through the second semester I was invited to give a series of lectures at another college, rather far down the academic pecking order compared to Todai. One of the young men in my class there perhaps disliked Todai and found it too smug for its own good, or maybe he just didn't care for foreigners; in any event, he used to look at me in a strangely dismissive way. He was well read and energetic – a far cry from many of his classmates, whose heads tended to droop towards the crooks of their elbows when they were no longer able to stay awake by finding things to laugh about or by fiddling with their mobile phones.

The young man in question had the disconcerting habit of staring at me with a look of unflinching scepticism. His face seemed to say "I'm here to learn something, but what you're telling me is either bollocks or boring." I felt that every word I uttered was being sifted through the fine filter of his merciless doubt, as though I were lecturing for him alone, summoning all the authority of my position in order to win a reprieve from his dismissive grimaces, and occasionally a nugget of grudging approval. At times he would frown as I made a point, darkly raise a single eyebrow – always a more menacing gesture than raising two – and jot down a note in a manner that was somehow both ostentatious and casual. His points, which were excellent, usually took the form of asking me how I reconciled one of my more obscure arguments with the even more obscure objections of some little-known thinker, and he was exceedingly well-briefed on the works of a great many little-known thinkers. After citing chapter and verse without consulting his notes, he would unleash his vicious question at me, accompanied by a look that said, "Try your hand at this one, pal!"

After a few weeks, as if initiating a new tactic with which to unsettle me, he took to giving me written notice by email of the following week's question, which of course made any sub-standard answer even less forgivable. He would request a "piece of comment" on the topic of his choice by the time of the next lecture, making it clear to me that he had only refrained from raising the matter in the last class in order to give me time to "prepare a convincing logical analysis".

A month or so into the course he also started cornering me after lectures. He would ask time-consuming follow-up questions, or seek laborious guidance on his career after graduating. I found these encounters unnerving – not because of his tenacious pursuit of me, which I actually quite admired, but because he became a completely different person. The cocky, bloodthirsty adversary of the class was replaced by a humble petitioner who verged on the obsequious – a "please could you possibly just help me with this minor point" kind of student. At first I thought there was only one explanation for this Jekyll and Hyde act. In the corridor after lectures he could be observed by his regular Japanese teachers, with whom the directness he employed with me was inconceivable; but in the classroom, freed of these constraints, he was trying to behave like a foreigner – which, for Japanese, often means an American. That required him, as I saw it, to be as combative as possible, almost a caricature of a sassy, individualistic, no-punches-pulled Texan. You frequently see this with Japanese: they so one-sidedly perfect the role of swaggering lone ranger who'll brook no nonsense from anyone that they become the sort of American who hardly exists – except in the movies or in the posturings of politicians. However, my analysis of his puzzling behaviour turned out to be off the mark.

One day, he caught up with me as I was leaving the classroom.

"Good afternoon Professor," he said, with overdone deference.

"You surely have a difficult question?" I teasingly answered.

"No, but have you got a moment?"

"Sure," I said. "You look unwell. Even ill. Have you got flu?"

"No, I often look like this. I am *so* badly nourished. I can't afford healthy food. Nourishment is my eternal problem."

His self-pity was cloying.

"But nourishment isn't my worst problem," he added quietly.

"Oh really? What…"

"I am in love."

"Well, that's wonderful," I said, feigning pleasure at this disastrous news, and feeling wary as to what he might want me to do with the information.

"It's affecting my work and my health."

"Is it?"

"It's really a bad situation."

"Is it? So how can I help?"

My stomach had been sinking, because I'd been half expecting him to ask me to mastermind the happy union; playing a *gaigin* matchmaker to this strange student and his inamorata was a role that could only have ended in a great deal of unintentional comedy or tragedy, or both.

"The problem is, she's the daughter of Professor X."

Professor X?

It slowly came to me – Professor X; he was the staff member who had sidled up to me after my second lecture. His distaste for my presence there was plain, his manner was ridiculing and his suspicion was paranoid. After a couple of hollow pleasantries he had paused, smiled mockingly, and asked me whether my real aim in visiting Japan was to "spy on our country". When I politely denied that, he had the gall to ask: "Then do you illegally trade gold?" After a further denial, he took a different tack, quizzing me about how I had come to teach at Todai and whether this meant that I was in fact in league with the "mafia of the Japanese State".

It took me forty-eight hours to become so irked by these questions and their bizarrely sarcastic manner that I had complained – "cheerfully" of course – to one of his colleagues. He gave me a perplexed smile for an answer and left it at that.

"What can I do?" my student was asking me, forlornly.

There was clearly no way I could – or would – intervene with Professor X to secure his daughter's hand for my inquisitorial student. Not wanting to discuss these matters in the corridor, where we might be overheard, I suggested that we repair to a nearby Starbucks. Over a pleasant coffee, I offered him a little pastoral advice, which he seemed to find helpful, but I also made it clear that intervention would be out of the question. As we took leave of each other afterwards, I was sure that our exchange had fostered a bond that would diminish his enthusiasm for punishing me with hard questions and sceptical stares.

But no: his public disdain for me was as uncompromising as ever, and he continued grilling me with abstruse and overly long philosophical enquiries. It was as if nothing had passed between us over our cup of coffee.

For several more weeks, I did my best to fulfil his requests for a "piece of comment", but he was openly dissatisfied with my responses. Most of his questions would have needed a full lecture to be answered properly, and the short replies I was forced to give carried the risk of discrediting me by seeming insufficiently comprehensive. I started to feel that he was getting the better of me psychologically, as if we were playing some unspoken and potentially lethal game of poker – which I sensed I was losing.

One day I snapped. It was the way he left the classroom, while I was still answering questions. He stood up menacingly, gathered his notes with pointed distaste, stuffed them into his briefcase, ambled arrogantly towards the door, turned round, gave me a look of breathtaking scorn, and walked out.

I wasn't prepared to accept this behaviour. I was furious that he was acting with such brazen contempt for me in front of the other students, especially since he had succeeded in seducing me into solicitous compassion for him by retailing his love pangs. So I regretfully interrupted another student's question, pursued him out of the room and confronted him in the corridor.

"Tell me what it is you don't understand," I started, feeling that my anger was at last endowing me with the necessary authority to turn the tables on him.

Far from being sheepish or backing down, he heightened the tension by simply staring at me with that same look of embittered scorn.

"Well?" I asked.

He looked ahead of him without blinking.

"I'm happy to meet you at any time to explain anything you don't understand."

"There are people who don't understand what you are doing here," he blurted, deadpan.

I was stunned. Here? At this college? In Tokyo? In Japan?

We stared at one other for some seconds, each of us summoning the inner strength to face down the other. Only pride prevented me from whacking him or storming off.

"That is extraordinarily rude," I finally spluttered, as I fantasized about booking a flight out of the country, or at least escaping back to the safe familiarity of Todai.

"I am not being rude: I am just talking frankly," he replied with astonishing level-headedness. "One of the professors seems to wonder what you are doing here," he added quietly, now staring at the floor.

"One of the professors?" I worried silently, imagining that hidden cliques of suspicion about me were stalking the corridors, spreading other rumours of which I was still unaware. All this also seemed completely at odds with the welcoming and warm treatment that I'd received at the college. Except, of course, for...

"Is it Professor X?" I asked him, instantly regretting the flash of concern that involuntarily crossed my face.

He wouldn't say.

"Well, anyway, I'm sorry," he muttered after a short pause, as if this were just a prank. "It really doesn't matter. I look forward to seeing you next week – whatever happens."

Whatever happens? What was going on? Had my student heard about Professor X's sarcastic interrogation of me and decided to ingratiate himself with his hoped-for father-in-law by discrediting me academically? Had Professor X even put him up to it? I could imagine the professor asking him to test whether I was simply posing as a philosopher, to find out whether I was actually a spy, a profiteer, an envoy of some foreign government intent on doing Japan down, or another unsavoury figment of the older man's imagination.

It seemed an unlikely coincidence to be treated like this by both the student and the father of the woman he loved. But having become a little more Japanese in my habits, the temptation to plump for this conspiracy theory was almost too hard to resist.

23

The Mecca of World Peace

If you're a nuclear tourist searching for traces of the Bomb, give Hiroshima a miss. This is a bustling, modern town with an overwhelming focus on the present and the future. In Hiroshima the past, for all its world-historical importance, really is another country – or, more accurately, another theme park. The theme park is about peace, and is managed for the benefit of two kinds of people: those who wish to remember – mostly foreigners – and those who wish to forget – mostly Japanese.

The foreigners, meaning primarily Americans, are there in order to inspect, regret, digest, or justify the reality of nuclear holocaust. Whatever their attitude to 6th August 1945, they want to smell the odour of history. They are hungry to face the horror of absolute destruction.

The Japanese are there less to confront reality than to sanitize it. To do this they have created one of Japan's most efficient mass-producers of virtual reality: the Peace Industry. This is an industry dedicated to forgetting. Its method is not to recall national crimes, as the Germans do, in order to say *nie wieder*; not to stare fascism's malign spirit in the face in

order to understand it and discredit it. Its method is to drill
the mantra of peace into the nation's mentality, so that it
becomes self-fulfilling. Not remembrance, but hypnosis.

If you want glimpses of the nightmare, there are only
two places to find it. One is the infinitely moving Peace
Memorial Museum, located near the Peace Bell and the
Peace Fountain in the Hiroshima Peace Park; the other is
the famous skeleton of the A-Bomb Dome – a monument
as much to Japan's survival as to its destruction. Almost all
the other evidence was bulldozed or silenced long ago.

The Dome – which topped the Industry Promotion Hall
before the mushroom fireball vaporized it – is, oddly, the less
powerful of the two memorials. Shorn of historical context,
it looks more maudlin than violated, more iconic than
real, a bit like one of those isolated ruins beloved of 19th-
century romantic artists such as Caspar David Friedrich. It
recalls the bombed-out church on Berlin's Kurfürstendamm,
the *Kaiser-Wilhelm-Gedächniskirche*, whose floodlit masonry
and jagged bell tower have become a reassuringly familiar
landmark, one of the few constants in a perpetually changing
urban environment, an epicentre of cosiness surrounded by
a popular open market, cafés and hotspots for late-night
assignations. Stripped of its history, just about everything
loses – or refuses – meaning.

In contrast to the Dome, the Peace Memorial Museum
is a gem: the simple, unsentimental way it shows the effects
of the Bomb on ordinary people and everyday life is
overwhelming. So is its roll-call of the horrors of all war.
Few of those horrors, however, are specifically attributed to
Japan. The Nazi death camps get their due, but I couldn't
find anything on Japanese prisoner-of-war camps – though
the Chinese and Korean forced labourers in war-time
Hiroshima are movingly commemorated. The war in

Vietnam is prominent, though it had nothing to do with Japan; while Japan's adventures in China and Korea, including the Rape of Nanking, are conspicuous by their absence. The devastation of the Atomic Bomb is everywhere, but the war in Asia that led to it is virtually nowhere. To some extent, this is inevitable: the museum is, after all, mainly about the realities of nuclear attack. There are sufficient other places to recall the larger historical picture.

And yet there is clearly denial at work here, the sort that is impervious to evidence or argument. The Japanese people and, in particular, the public bureaucracies – which exert an iron control over the museums for which they are responsible, as well as over schools and textbooks and other agents of remembrance – have never come to terms with the evil of the fascist policies of the 1930s. The criminal acts of a perverted regime and national spirit have not been confronted to even a fraction of the extent that Germans have so courageously managed. Most Japanese regard the whole historical episode as foolish rather than unethical; or, even worse, as nevertheless somehow "pure", insofar as it was courageous and unhesitating and patriotic. Some even see Japan's Asian War as an entirely legitimate attempt to stem the tide of Westernization that threatened the unique Japanese soul and all of Asia's identity.

In any event, few apologies have been forthcoming, and even by a Japanese conception of sincerity – doing wholeheartedly what is expected of you in any particular situation – the apologies that have been made don't seem particularly sincere. But sincere apologies for other sorts of errors happen all the time, for example in cases of corporate failure, or when financial or medical scams get discovered. Unconditional apology is very much part of the Japanese tradition. So is the belief that something is bad if it fails, and very bad if it fails very badly.

I had a strange sense of deprivation, of an unnatural and corrosive silence all around me, as the city that inaugurated the nuclear era stubbornly refused to yield any further evidence or explanation of the Bomb. It seemed incredible to be standing in this place whose name resonated in every corner of the globe, and yet to feel as though I were in the middle of a gigantic cover-up. Obliteration had itself been obliterated. In its stead stood the "Mecca of World Peace", as one brochure had it: just another ugly Japanese town, with the ubiquitous overhead cables and tangles of roads and soulless boxlike buildings and unplanned chaos. As I wandered the bustling streets, I couldn't help wondering how a nation so innately receptive to beauty could live amid such atrocious ugliness. The Japanese seem in love, above all, with the *idea* of beauty, their feeling for beauty having become so abstract that it doesn't necessarily find expression in actual things. Where beauty undeniably exists, it tends to be either portable or ephemeral – as it is in food, in ceramics, in traditional dress, in contemporary clothes, in horticulture.

Tired and hungry – by now the Peace Museum and the Dome seemed like tiny islands where the past was prohibited from flowing into the present or the future – I plumped for a simple café serving delicious-smelling *hoto dogos* (hot dogs). I ordered an espresso, and was leafing through a *Herald Tribune* that another nuclear pilgrim must have left behind when I was interrupted by a mousy voice.

"Excuse me," she said. Then, a little more boldly: "Excuse me if you please."

A small lady, perhaps in her early fifties, with sparkling eyes and dyed jet-black hair done up into a scraggy bun, was bending over me.

"I like foreigners," she said. "Foreigners good people."

I thanked her for her approval, and hastened to resume

my reading, suspecting that she was a chatterbox who had never terminated a conversation of her own free will.

"You like Japanese? We good people? What's your sense of us?"

I smiled affirmatively, mainly because I meant it, but also to avoid a dialogue from which I would be unable to extricate myself.

"What do you do?" she persisted.

"Guess," I succumbed.

"Construction engineer. Or maybe computer software. Anyway, something very modern. You look like a very modern man."

"Terrible insight," I teased her. She loved that, and was now definitely coming back for more.

"Good husband. Maybe good lover."

"Wrong again."

"Politician? No, you too nice man for politician. And maybe not rich enough."

"Philosopher," I replied. "Closely connected to good lover," I added purely to wind her up.

"Of course!" she said. "Plato *eros*. I love Plato *eros*. You can feel it everywhere."

"And what do you do?" I asked.

"I own beauty salon," she answered triumphantly.

I was really warming to her. And even if I hadn't been, she wouldn't have left me in peace. She was determined to converse, get under the skin of a foreigner, and brush up or show off her impressive English.

"What does your beauty salon do?" I asked.

"So!" she said decisively, trying to summon up all the relevant English words and arrange them into the right order: "Manicure, pedicure, massage, facial beauty, and of course coiffeur. I make people very relaxing!"

"Do you do men?"

"No… But for you… Yes." She giggled and stroked my shoulder. "If you teach me some Kanto."

"Kant isn't very relaxing," I said, impressed that she had heard of him. "Neither to teach nor to learn. I've just given a course on his ethics at Todai."

Perhaps emboldened by the reception of this magic word by the Yamazaki family in the Nagano Alps, I was testing what response I would get in Hiroshima.

"Ah! Todai! You are at Todai?"

The way she lingered on the "o" of Todai was admiring but hesitant. I could see I wasn't in for outright adulation.

"But Todai so old-fashioned. You think really good for today Japan? Just manufacture more bureaucrats, who build more bridges and roads and concrete, and destroy Japan natural beauty. And steal so much money." And she affected a look of mock worry.

This woman was altogether more subtle than met the eye.

"How can philosopher at Todai eat *hoto dogo*?" she demanded, looking pityingly at the wretched sausage streaked with mustard and ketchup. "You are typical American!"

"But Japanese must like it," I said. "No one else here is foreign."

"Japan going to the dogs," she said. "To the *hoto dogs*," she added, laughing at her own pun. "Maybe Japan finished!" – a phrase I had heard so often that it now numbed rather than alarmed me. I knew what was coming: "Too much American influence. Essence of Japanese special soul disappearing. Unique relationship to nature lost. And so economic strength of Japan also lost. Our Japanese blood no longer pure."

Mercifully, she kept this refrain brief. But her laments followed the usual pattern: Japan was losing a unique soul formed in the mists of ancestral time. This soul was sincere, genuine, resilient, uncompromising and had a wholesome relationship to nature and the gods. It was being undermined by superficial foreign influences, mainly American culture, epitomized by fast food and aggressive individualism. And with the loss of its traditional virtues, Japan was no longer strong enough to beat the West at its own game.

Then abruptly, more like a command than an offer:

"Well, now I invite you to stay at my apartment for as long as you want. Cancel hotel and stay with me. I promise not to talk all the time!"

If she hadn't promised, I might have believed her. But this pre-emptive reassurance confirmed that she was a seasoned conversational warrior who wouldn't easily fall silent.

We caught a bus to her place, a poky apartment in Western style. The hall was so narrow that I almost had to edge down it sideways. She took me into the kitchen-diner, which could just about accommodate dinner for two across a table the size of a chessboard. There was a faint whiff of leaking gas coming from the canister that serviced the single-ring hob of a camping cooker. An old fridge that would have been at home in a design museum of Fifties domestic appliances was flanked by rows of light-green laminated cabinets. The corridor also gave onto two other rooms; each of them had little space for anything but a bed jammed between the walls and an aluminium rail for hanging clothes on.

Lodged in such a homely space with a kind stranger from Hiroshima, it seemed an ideal moment to speak to an ordinary resident of the city about the Bomb and its legacy.

"We Japanese are fundamentally very peaceful people," she replied, not answering my questions. "We never want war, against nobody. Korea and China still don't understand how much we love peace. They always getting excited about history." She poured me a cup of green tea. "So! That's it. Enough of Bomb talk! Enough of nuclear things! They belong to Japan past; they out of date now. I went on home stay to America many years ago, and people only want to talk with me about Hiroshima bomb. Why? Such uncheerful talk."

She paused. "Anyway, Bomb was America's crime, though they say it was necessary to end World War. Japanese military government crimes, Stalin crimes, American Hiroshima crimes – all the same! What difference? Just very bad times!"

It shocked me, but oddly it didn't surprise me, her statement that America's Atomic Bomb, Stalin's Gulag and Japan's Rape of Asia were all morally equivalent. Was it a conviction or merely a hazy mantra?

"Well, I must go to wedding reception this afternoon. So please make yourself at home." Then, after a moment's thought: "Would you like to come with me?"

"Oh, I'd love to!" I replied enthusiastically, leaping at the opportunity to be part of a Japanese wedding. "But I haven't got a suit or anything."

"No problem, you take my son's! He will give you. You're welcome. And you take his invitation card, if you please," she added.

"I'm, um, probably too large for his clothes." I had visions of trousers extending no further than my calves, and of a pair of Western shoulders splitting the seams of the jacket.

She led me to the messy little cubbyhole that was her son's bedroom, and rummaged around on the coat rail. "By the way, you sleep here," she said. "My son away working for Toshiba company." It looked like a teenager's bedroom, full of posters of Western rock idols and Japanese models dressed in flimsy, cut-away dresses, and with cigarette ash trodden into the tatty carpet.

I tried on a badly cut, light-grey salaryman's suit which she fished out of a jumble of old clothes. I was right about the shoulders, and wrong about the calves. The jacket was far too narrow, but the sleeves and legs were comically long, tailored for a gangly youth who would tower over me. I could imagine her son from the cut of his suit and the unkempt asceticism of his room: gaunt, bony and lank.

"Next, you need gift, if you please. Maybe 20,000 Yen. Yes, for stranger only 20,000 Yen necessary. I'm sorry but weddings in Japan so expensive that guests must give money to pay for banquet and gifts that we receive at ceremony." And she fetched a beautifully creased envelope, into which she inserted two crisp 10,000 Yen bills of her own money.

Refusing this generosity, I immediately fished two of my own out of my trouser pocket.

She cracked up laughing: "You can't possibly give that! No, no, impossible! In Japan, we present only fresh new bills from bank, never used ones, even in good condition." And she buried her face in her hands and squeaked with amusement, still pointing at my crumpled bills. "They look terrible! So terrible! Must sound like this to be correct." And she flicked one of her bills in that deft, snappy way of checkout clerks and sales people throughout Japan. I found the sound of crisp bills being flicked like that oddly satisfying.

After much resistance, she accepted my bills and gave me the envelope with hers. Examining it more closely, I noticed that it was really two envelopes, an inner wrapper meticulously folded around the bills, and an outer decorated with a printed red-and-white ribbon and sprigs of pine. As one would expect from a culture obsessed with form and appearance, Japan has a complex semiotics of wrapping, the quality of which is unsurpassed anywhere in the world. Protocol dictates precisely what type of envelope and form of address to use for each occasion, from ordinary mail to cards and gifts for weddings, births, funerals, New Year and the whole calendar of festivals. As in so much of Japanese life, appearance is inseparable from content. Form *is* reality; surface *is* substance.

We jumped into a taxi called "Cedric" and drove to the local wedding palace, inching our way through the traffic jams of this bustling city that had so inelegantly but decisively resurrected itself from total destruction.

24

Gate-crashing in Hiroshima

The squat, rectangular building boasted a vast doorway shaped like a triumphal arch, which was flanked by two pageboys in European courtly costume holding trumpets at the ready. The large foyer was studded with long conical electric lanterns around its walls, and decked out with chintzy sofas, mauve satin armchairs, mock-Chippendale cabinets, rushed curtains, sparkling chandeliers, and other icons of *kitschy* comfort. A queue of people waiting to register their arrival, gifts in hand, snaked around the milling guests. In return for our little envelopes of money we were each presented with a bag containing a tiny melon, a kilo of rice, dried fish, a porcelain bowl and some chocolates, which we deposited at the cloakroom with our coats. I noticed that my new friend's envelope had genuine, rather than printed, ribbons, and that a strip of abalone was glued to the top right-hand corner. Mine must have been the economy version.

After a lot of waiting, the sound of trumpets signalled the arrival of the bride and groom and their attendant family members. They drew up in two polished black rickshaws, drawn by bronzed young men with perfectly sculpted bodies, wearing traditional kimono-style short jackets over black shirts and tights. Everyone clapped enthusiastically as the newly-weds cautiously descended from their high perch, each assisted by a tugging Adonis, and walked gingerly down the red carpet of the foyer, glancing left and right but not really looking at anyone. Both were sombre to the point of impassiveness as they made their stately progress towards a set of ornamental doors that led to the ballroom beyond. He was dressed in a male kimono of black silk and *hakama* loose-fitting trousers, secured with an spotless white sash. She wore the customary white bridal kimono, with its winglike sleeves embroidered with peacocks and other birds of paradise. Her face was powdered waxen-white, and a geisha's red lipstick traced the lines of her mouth, so that you could detect the smallest movement of her lips. A large hood reached high like a canopy over her ornate hairdo, whose graceful sweep was decorated with tiny flowers and jewels. This elaborate headgear supposedly hides the "horns of jealousy" that all new wives are expected to sprout, evidently within minutes of taking their nuptial vows – an expectation that struck me as typically Japanese in its down-to-earth realism. Japanese men are, with good reason, deeply terrified of female jealousy, and well practised at feigning coolness when confronted with it. It is a myth that wives calmly accept philandering husbands as part of a "deal" in which she gets social status, income and children while he is granted a second mother and sexual freedom. Though wives can't do much about it, because of the social ignominy still attached to divorce, their anger, active and passive, is alive and kicking.

The solemnity of the couple's bearing conveyed something wonderfully pristine: a quiet and natural respect for tradition, or imagined tradition. This was in violent contrast to the sugary contrivances of the foyer and ballroom, with their pot-pourri of naff furnishings and clichés of luxury plagiarized pell-mell from Western suburbia. As they approached the ballroom, the crowd rapidly closed in behind them, funnelling through the ornate doorway into the large dim space like a great fish tail vanishing into the sea. In the crush the two families were finally forced to succumb to proximity, and to abandon the separate phalanxes into which they had, until then, been resolutely divided.

Squeezing through the doorway with the last curious stragglers, I saw bride and groom emerge from a side room, now in less formal kimonos. To polite applause, they walked ceremonially around the four sides of the ballroom, greeting their guests, before mounting a platform to join a dozen or so family, friends and business colleagues. At no point did they exchange the slightest sign of affection. Meanwhile, attention was riveted on the long buffet table in the middle of the room, towards which many of the three hundred or so guests were insistently gravitating. Few were listening to the speeches by the two fathers, the groom's boss, child-hood and college friends, and the "matchmaker" (who, my new friend told me, was paid to fake his traditional role of "arranging" the marriage, though, in fact, the couple had met on an Internet dating site). Most of the guests were forming an orderly but firm scrum, three or four deep, around the buffet.

The end of the decidedly unfunny speeches – replete with clichés about happiness, destiny and love, and discreet stories of the bride and groom's past – unleashed a feeding frenzy of barely veiled brutality. Almost at once people started barging their way to the food table. The choicest offerings, like a plate of gleaming lobster tails placed invitingly on little shelves of sculpted ice, were hoovered

up first, as guests ripped plastic films off the dishes they
coveted before bemused waitresses had even been given the
order to do so. A particularly fierce knot of greed formed
around a chef who was continually cooking fresh pasta.
Conversation, bowing and greeting dried up completely,
as formerly milling guests turned themselves into a huge
lattice of grabbing arms, straining bodies and avaricious
eyes. By the time I made it to the table, a forlorn succession
of empty plates, strewn with unwanted lettuce leaves and
tomato segments, was all that remained of the expensive
Western food, while bowls bursting to the brim with salads
and cold meat stood conspicuously untouched. In addition,
a mouth-watering selection of sushi and sashimi lay inexplicably intact; and I gorged myself on this fantastically
fresh fish, amazed and delighted at the lack of competition
that I encountered.

I have always counted myself among the very best
when it comes to attacking a buffet, having honed over
many years the skill of carefully inspecting a spread, casually moving in on the best bits, and then striking with
unhesitating decisiveness. But on this occasion I found
unexpected inspiration from the Japanese, who seemed to
dispense with the stage of nonchalant hovering and instead
went directly for the kill, edging each other out of the way
with impeccably polite vehemence. People were seizing
the delicacies by any means available: sticking in their forks,
if the serving spoons were being used by others; stabbing
the food with their knives; and if all else failed using their
hands, sometimes both. Many of those who hadn't secured
ring-side positions were reaching between feeders who
were closer to the action, dripping gravy onto the starched
table clothes or smudging cocktail sauce over the suits and
kimonos of front-row predators. These gluttons had one

clear advantage over Westerners in a similar situation: if they roughly displaced someone from the front line or else hogged a particularly desirable morsel just as another guest was about to claim it for himself, the victim couldn't show he'd noticed, let alone that he was furious; or else both parties would have lost face. The danger of getting one's comeuppance was much more remote than in a Western culture, where the baser forms of rapaciousness can be openly reprimanded.

The bride and groom had eaten nothing at all; they had been too busy talking to the speakers on the platform – and being photographed by a man with a huge camera on a tripod who seemed to take more or less the same shot of them over and over again – to pick from the food that a waitress had rescued for them. And then they had vanished, though barely any of the guests could have noticed.

Suddenly the lights went down, casting the war zone of barren tables into welcome darkness, and powerful beams of red, yellow and blue light projected a myriad tiny zig-zagging hearts onto the walls. As the kaleidoscopic images raced and wriggled over the room, a second surprise raised the overdue suspense another notch. At the end of the ballroom opposite the platform, two great doors opened and a huge tiered wedding cake, a good two metres high, was rolled in to the sounds of Elvis singing 'Love Me Tender'.

Bride and groom glided in on the same platform, dwarfed by the cake, together clutching a giant knife in the shape of a samurai sword, which glinted menacingly in the moving beams. Both had changed their clothes yet again, she into a glittering ball gown, he into a tuxedo. As the song climaxed, they raised the knife high above their heads and, with help from two waiters, brought it down onto the first layer of the monster cake – which lit up translucently, revealing a star-spangled interior and a merry-go-round of angels on horseback.

This stunt unleashed wild applause and had obviously been secretly planned by the bride's family, because no one looked more amazed than the groom. Small step ladders were immediately provided by the waiters, and the couple were asked to mount them in order to make their next attempt at cutting the cake, this time on its second tier. Up they clambered, and down came the sword. But this, too, yielded only another illumination, now bearing the names of bride and groom in neon-lit kanji, flanked by little rococo cupids. It was going to be a case of third-time lucky. And as they brought the sword down on the third tier, it sunk reassuringly into the heart of the cake. Waving stiffly to the cheering audience, the groom expressed suitably humble surprise at the trick that had been played on him, and then they sealed their success with their "first kiss", while Elvis was still crooning his approval.

The official cutting and kissing over, waiters armed with more step ladders hurried to prepare a slice for every guest and, with that ineffably deft service of the Japanese, driven by total dedication to the task in hand, three hundred people duly received a perfectly presented piece of cake. After toasts to the couple, the groom, in his reply, related in oleaginous detail how they would eat a small portion every day until they conceived their first child, and added that the centre of the cake was to be reserved for this infant and his or her siblings. Finally, with the formalities over, loudspeakers blared out Cole Porter's 'True Love', and the newly-weds' poker-faced composure, relentlessly sustained even through their official kiss, abruptly gave way to relaxed intimacy and to luminous joy in each other.

Sitting down at a little table in the ballroom, I asked my new friend about the love of her own life. This didn't feel odd: women in Japan can be astoundingly open – much more so than men.

"In my day, marriage was arranged by parents," she said. "But I was lucky: I love my husband and he love me. But he die three years ago. This really help me love him more."

I asked her what she called love.

"Of course, every couple become bored of each other from time to time. That's normal. But my husband always give me sense of my identity. And so he give me sense of my value. For me, love always give sense of value. Otherwise, it is no love."

"But when we give a sense of value to people, don't we always try to change them into someone more accessible to us, almost out of love, so that we can value them even more?"

"Yes, of course, that is temptation for everybody. But when my husband value me, he just protect my identity. He defend my soul, but he never try to change it. And certainly not to possess it."

"That's very hard. Not many people can do that."

"I know. I try to do same for my husband, but perhaps I always try to reform something about him! Always try to keep him for myself!" And clenching her fists she hugged an imaginary figure.

"So tell me how he defended your soul."

"Just through his simple presence. Just by looking at me."

"Did he defend you by trying to heal past suffering, or to give you courage when you felt vulnerable?"

"No, not really. He was just present for me. Without words. Without making a deal. Without expecting anything in return."

"And fidelity?"

"I don't know. Fidelity not so important as Western people say. Many years ago, Japanese wife like to send husband for evening of pleasure with geisha, and even dress him up to look nice for geisha, and then settle bill for his visit. But still husband and wife could protect each other soul!"

Next morning I left Hiroshima. It had been a strange visit, which had denied me the expected immersion in nuclear tourism and instead exposed me, at close quarters, to emotions such as love and friendship that, contrary to myth, the Japanese have in as much abundance as any Western nation. Food, marriage, new relationships – time present and future – had invaded the territory that I had thought would be dominated by time past. And so it usually is in today's Japan.

25

KAISEKI AND THE BAKED POTATO

As the bullet train from Hiroshima pulled into Kyoto station, on its way back to Tokyo, I took a snap decision to jump off there and then, in order to see the sublime Ryoan-ji rock garden again and try to reserve a couple of nights at the fabled Tawaraya Inn, sometimes called the world's best hotel. I was allowing myself an almost carnal indulgence in the tranquil majesty of old Japan: the misty gardens, hanging scrolls, silent temples and gently splashing waterfalls. I had deliberately resisted this numinous world so far, because I'd been determined to plunge into today's Japan rather than submit to the surviving relics of its incomparable but dying heritage. I had feared, too, that once I was enveloped in pristine silence, order and emptiness, the loud, chaotic, cluttered world of contemporary Japan would become altogether too monotonous to inhabit.

It was off-season, mid-week, and the Tawaraya had a room for two nights – fortunately, because you usually need to book months in advance, and perhaps unfortunately, because there was a price tag upwards of $2,000. Of this, around $1,000 would be for the two dinners. No matter: from the moment I'd arrived in this land of heavenly gastronomy, I'd decided to put my mouth where my money was. I'd spent at least half my professor's salary on food, and had seldom regretted a penny of it.

All of classical Japan is compacted into this extraordinary Inn, or *ryokan,* on a Kyoto backstreet: refinement of the highest order; the bewitching art of understatement; service so subtle that, for the most part, it is invisible; the voluptuousness of solitude as well as its terrors; the unseen and ultimately unseeable world of the inner life. For this is a hotel with no driveway, no lobby, no gym, no restaurants, no bars, indeed with no public spaces at all except for the beautifully kept inner gardens, a miniscule "library" which is usually empty, and a labyrinth of corridors where each turn greets you with an exquisite surprise: a flower arrangement in a simple ceramic vase, a folding screen depicting a mountain scene in the Zen style of brush painting, or a little bamboo spout dripping water serenely into a stone basin. Life here happens in your room and on your own. In two nights and two days, I didn't meet another guest, though the used trays outside other rooms confirmed that I wasn't alone. This pinnacle of traditional luxury is not easy to take for modern senses accustomed to continual avalanches of stimulation. Here you have to attune yourself to the intensity of sparseness.

Elegy out of precision. The perfection of my room was breathtaking: the impeccably brushed *tatami* matting; the alcove with hanging plant, incense dish and scroll; the private garden outside a large glass window, where an old gardener was weeding and watering with miniature, almost ingrown, movements; the large antique lacquered table; the legless *za-isu* chairs either side of the table, each with a single brocaded armrest; a cedar bath tub evincing the most delicate fragrance; the sensuous magic of the polished white wood pillars, partly inlaid into the wall. Modern conveniences, such as telephone and television, were covered with starched white cloth or else stowed in tiny, low cupboards. I had hardly a moment to inspect this panorama of purity when my kimonoed maid brought in green tea with the choicest sweet and bitter aromas to refresh me. In the Tawaraya no wants are left unattended, even if you aren't yet aware of them.

Though I could have lingered for hours in this slow, silent, spare world that allowed imagination and time such free rein, and where modesty verged on the immodest, the day was too beautiful to stay indoors. A relay of whispers must have announced my departure to the elderly doorman, for exactly as I approached the lanterned entrance, he brought my shoes out for me, freshly polished, placing them neatly on a washed flagstone and standing by to help me with a shoehorn. A moment later, a taxi whisked me off to Ryoan-ji temple, the doorman and my maid bowing low in the street until we turned the corner and left their sight.

Intensely personal and intensely anonymous: this is also the signature of the Zen rock garden at Ryoan-ji, one of the greatest masterpieces of world art and, for me, the only place on earth where the sacred cannot be abused. Everywhere else where the sacred manifestly lives there is latent power to justify fanaticism, self-righteousness, contempt for those outside the magic circle. One need think only of the holy places and books of Christianity, Islam and Judaism, or even pure nature, like the enchanted forests of Germany, Poland and Russia. But who would kill in the name of fifteen irregularly shaped rocks with no agreed – or even definable – meaning? Who would justify a murderous ideology on the basis of their enigmatic spatial relationships and their furry tufts of moss? Who would be inspired by a sea of raked white gravel to dehumanize and subdue foreign peoples? Unlike a god who saves, chooses or dies for the faithful, unlike a mythology that elevates one nation or creed above all others, there is nothing here to inspire violence, hubris, or condemnation. Any such feelings fall on stony ground in this most magnificent of "dry landscape" gardens. Its rocks and moss and gravel voicelessly refuse explanations or justifications. They are pregnant with meaning; but none that can be articulated.

Crucial to the power of the rock garden is the low earthen wall which marks it off from the thrusting pine, cedar and cherry trees outside its perimeter that tower over, but never invade, its space. This wall, itself a masterpiece of proportion, borders the rectangular garden on three sides and is overhung by a narrow-beamed wooden roof. It represents not just the demarcation between inner and outer, between the unfamiliar, man-made rock garden and the more familiar ordering of nature surrounding it; the wall, with its clear dimensions and functions, contrasts starkly with the rock garden that, for all its order and its everyday items like moss and gravel, evokes a realm of awareness beyond borders and fixity. This is a realm of freedom where our consciousness is almost palpably refined, provided we can sustain an attentiveness that really *looks*.

Drawn into contemplation of the Zen garden, we see how the world of spirit and the world of things, the transcendental and the profane, the sublime and the everyday, are ultimately inseparable. The spiritual is not superior to the real, or distinct from the everyday. The spiritual *is* the everyday intensely felt (and then, perhaps, expressed in thought and art and religion and the like). It is how we would experience the real if we could maximally open ourselves to it. If, that is, we had the courage, empathy and persistence for such openness. Far from discrediting the idea of the spiritual – the urge to do so is myopic and narrowing – Ryoan-ji shows that a fully human relation to the world is spiritual through and through; that the more we allow the raw presence of things and their relationships to speak, the more we will experience them as spiritual in their very essence. As a result any conception of human life that does not flow from and embody this passionate and compassionate openness to the world does not deserve the name "spiritual"; and all doctrines that oppose the spiritual to the worldly or the human are bogus and vain.

Yet the closer we approach the reality of anything, and so its spirituality, the more surely we will experience its ultimate remoteness. The paradox is that only as we gain the bliss of intimacy with things – a rock, a person, a god – do we encounter the terror of their ungraspable solipsism. In attaining the personal, we always come up against the impersonal. And vice versa: in *really* confronting the impersonal we necessarily enter into the personal. There is no deep relationship, therefore, that is wholly personal and wholly intimate. (Perhaps this is why the divine is unattainable: not because it is a fiction but, on the contrary, because it is the final reality, and so is the most profoundly ungraspable and impersonal of all realities. Perhaps, too, this is why many of us refuse the divine: not because it can't be proved – many beliefs we accept can't be proved – but because we are repelled by its ultimate inaccessibility and wish to experience *only* its intimate and personal aspect. Yet such one-sidedness is impossible.)

The shadows were lengthening in the enchanted garden, the crowds of tourists and schoolchildren were thinning, and eventually I found myself, for a minute or two, alone in the dim light and in complete silence. I sat facing the brooding rocks, submitting to their nameless wisdom, and sensing, for a second here and there, that vivid but ineffable sense of eternity which the Western mind will never cease to crave. (And which will never be overcome merely by deciding to affirm everything temporal, ephemeral, partial, novel, and supposedly opposed to it.) Eventually a monk politely indicated that it was closing time, and I realized that dinner at the Tawaraya awaited me at precisely 6.00 p.m., as did my German friend Sophie whom I had invited to join me. I took one last look at the still masterpiece, exhausted and exhilarated by the attentiveness it demanded. It abruptly withdrew its presence the moment I ceased to attend to it with the active passivity, the taut receptivity to which alone it would yield. Slightly saddened by its retreat, but also a little relieved to be freed of its power, I left swiftly for the *ryokan*.

Curiosity for the impending banquet must have overtaken me because, as my taxi sped through Kyoto, passing innumerable magnificent temples that I wouldn't have time to see, I started to blank out the tremendous richness of this city, which is birthplace to so much of the country's religion, literature, ceramics and theatre. Just as in one's teens, sex can suddenly swamp and blur one's entire vision, so now I felt this heady mixture of promise, desire, escape and fear at my first encounter with the complexities of *kaiseki ryori*, the haute cuisine of Kyoto and the most refined in Japan, if not in the world.

The only problem was that I was really hungry – not a condition to be recommended when eating *kaiseki*. The total calorific value of its ten to twenty courses, each of which provides only a bite or two though it might take many hours to prepare, possibly equals that of a modest sandwich. So I had the taxi stop at a roadside stall on the way, for a packet of peanuts and some tangerines, in case my appetite got too stimulated by dinner. Tucking them into the inside pocket of my coat, I plucked up courage to be welcomed back at the Tawaraya, preparing myself not to be intimidated by the staff's unflinching attentiveness, and organizing my possessions so that they would leave the taxi with me in one piece. It seemed self-evident that the doorman would divine my imminent arrival, and be waiting expectantly outside the entrance, as if for me alone, with that benign vigilance which permanently marked his bearing.

Which of course he was. As the taxi drew up to the Inn, visible in the gathering darkness only by its soft lanterns, I saw him in silhouette, stooped and immobile like an aged sentry. My preparations for a dignified exit paid off: I managed to avoid my usual tendency to rummage chaotically around the back seat for plastic bags, gloves, guidebooks, keys and loose coins; or, worse still, to grab my coat the wrong way up and send everything flying out of the pockets. As I lumbered out, the smiling figure of my maid was waiting just inside the entrance to relieve me of these encumbrances – though I made sure she didn't see the peanuts and the tangerines. Shoes whisked away by the doorman, I found myself back in the stillness of my room, with its garden veranda gently floodlit and the low lacquered table set for dinner.

As soon as Sophie arrived, the ceremony began. Nothing is deeply experienced unless one encounters it at the right pace; and *kaiseki* is no exception. The procession of dishes was perfectly timed and the whole was imbued with magical harmony. In fact, with five sorts of harmony. There was harmony of colour. Second, harmony of raw texture – for uncooked ingredients. Third, harmony of added texture, imparted by the four methods of cooking represented in our dinner: stewing, steaming, grilling, and shallow-frying. Fourth, harmony of landscape, balancing the flavours of mountain, plain, river and sea. And, finally, harmony of salty, sweet, sour, bitter and sharp.

After a couple of days on this sort of diet, the challenge of soon reverting to Western food seemed daunting. The thought of a slab of steak, or a mass of starchy pasta, or a dismembered vein- and nerve-riddled chicken carcass, or the pungent, burly flavours of so much Western cooking in general, was perfectly disgusting. So was using such brutal implements as knives and forks, which, unlike disposable chopsticks, release oxidized metal into your food and, in restaurants, have been in thousands of other mouths. I was even coming to share the horror of my Japanese friends at my morning muesli, which they regarded as little better than animal feed, or wood shavings or – after pouring milk over it – soggy peat. It was good, therefore, to be returning to Tokyo for a couple of weeks, as a sort of gastronomic quarantine before flying back to Europe. I resolved to stick to simple foods in order to ease the transition: soba noodles, yakitori chicken, tofu, soups of vegetable and shrimp. Though this basic fare was delicious, it was less traumatic to forego than, say, sushi, sukiyaki, fugu, Zen-temple food, *kaiseki*, and the other higher reaches of what is possibly the greatest living tradition of gastronomy on the planet.

As the bullet train streaked back to Tokyo, I also decided that despite my new disgust for Western foods, I had to face my fear: the swiftest way to wean myself off Japanese food would be to mount sporadic, violent and sustained attacks on the palate using such taste bombs as pasta with gorgonzola and smoked-ham sauce, triple-decker sandwiches mixing cheese, meat and pickles, double-chocolate muffins and strong coffee. Under such duress, my taste buds would become sufficiently numbed and disoriented to stop craving the unavailable. And after a fortnight of corrective training, it was true that I was duly capable of eating a small meal in London from beginning to end without feeling abused. Sometimes, the only solution to losing something is to overwhelm yourself with its opposite.

When I got back to Tokyo, I asked Yuki what she would do in my situation.

"I recommend baked potato in Cotswold district of England. Best baked potato in the world. I never ate a potato like it. One has missed something unique until one eat Cotswold baked…"

I interrupted her and taught her the phrase "damning with faint praise". She didn't quite get it until I remarked that Japanese often judge foreigners benignly, by rock-bottom standards which they wouldn't be seen dead applying to themselves.

She vigorously denied this. "Please, Simon, I'm serious. The Cotswold baked potato 100% unbeatable. I even went into the kitchen and asked chef how he make such a thing. I think you need a special sort of potato, special sort of oven. So far I haven't managed to copy it."

After nearly a year here, I was no longer fazed by the deftness of Japanese condescension. The put-downs are so playfully deadpan that they're hard to counter. It was perfectly obvious that the story of the baked potato referred more to Yuki's horror of anglophone cooking than to the perfection of the world's crudest vegetable.

"Well, of course," Yuki admitted, after my needling finally punctured her rituals of admiration, "I feel sorry for English people. Cotswold baked potato is great, but otherwise your food is so bad, it might be better to give it to your animals. Then, at least, they would be healthy."

It turned out she was referring to mad-cow disease.

This reminded me to tell her the old adage that the English kill their beef twice: once when they slaughter the animal and once when they cook it. "And a third time when they feed it," she added for good measure.

The amusement that many Japanese derive from trawling over the supposed awfulness of English and American cooking – indeed of most foreign cooking except French, Italian and Chinese – masks genuine disbelief, even terror, at its concoctions.

"One of my best friends," Yuki said, "distinguished chef, visit England recently and on his return he try reassure me that English cooking isn't as bad as we Japanese think; in fact, that it's made lot of progress. But I don't believe. Copying French, Italian or Japanese technique, or mixing them all up, will not produce anything genuine, especially if there isn't great history to draw on. You would be better to stick to simple thing, like Cotswold baked potato."

For Yuki the baked potato was all that stood between English food and gastronomic barbarity. Her attitude reminded me of Bernard Shaw's quip that America was the only country ever to have gone from barbarism to decadence without passing through civilization. But then Shaw also believed that Stalin's Soviet Union was a triumph of human civilization.

26

The Bureaucrats' Long Goodbye

Saying goodbye can be hardest when love is unrequited. Though the Japanese are wonderfully loyal, hospitable, courteous and kind, they seldom reciprocate a foreigner's *love*. Affection, obligation, fascination, generosity, respect – yes. But love – no.

This is partly because as a foreigner you really are seen as incurably "other" – more so than almost anywhere else in the world. There is no halfway house, as between Western countries, or between the West and, say, India, where people accept that a foreigner can engage with a different cultural heritage. The Japanese manage to feel utterly distinct from everyone else, including other Asians like the Koreans and Chinese who have nourished Japan's own culture for at least fifteen centuries. They persuade themselves that although they can fathom other cultures, other cultures cannot fathom theirs. Nothing a foreigner can do can finally overcome this belief. Like anyone in a state of entrenched belief, they have ceased to listen.

Nor, incidentally, should a foreigner *try* to overcome this belief. The worst strategy for success in Japan, apart from being openly conflictual, is to ape their manners too scrupulously, with too much stiff bowing, pensive muttering and feigned surprise. Even learning Japanese fluently isn't necessarily a good idea. You should learn it well, but not too well, or else you might look like a Trojan horse. It is part of the *gaigin*'s etiquette to live up to Japanese clichés of the foreigner, to "be oneself" at all times, to parade one's otherness – if necessary, by acting the alien.

Unfortunately, being cast as intrinsically "other" makes it *impossible* to be loved. Or even to be fully trusted. And this kills the deep attentiveness, the pure receptivity, that is the basis of all love. "Ultimately, we Japanese prefer the company of other Japanese to the company of foreigners," a distinguished international businessman told me as he invited me to a magnificent sushi dinner. "However much we enjoy and value our foreign friends, we feel really comfortable only with our own people." He was a widely travelled man, interested and educated in other cultures, with two children at school in the United States and with homes in London and New York. Most people share his attitudes.

The sudden social death that I experienced at Todai after my professorship came to an end – when, with three or four touching exceptions, my living presence seemed to be summarily erased from the hearts of those students and colleagues who bore me undoubted affection – was easily my most painful experience in Japan. Though I had enjoyed warm relations throughout the year with both graduates and undergraduates, only three students bothered to turn up to my leaving dinner. And none gave me a parting gift of any sort. This was particularly striking in a country so powerfully governed by obligations towards those who have helped you and by complex rules of gift-giving aimed at achieving precise reciprocity for favours rendered. Worst of all, when I turned up to my students' graduation ceremonies at the end of March, a month after the end of the previous semester, I felt like a stranger, an unnoticed shadow consigned to the past, without presence or significance. Social obligations, at least in this situation, clearly lasted only as long as social roles: theirs of student, mine of professor. As my year drew to an end, so too did our relationship and its duties. I was left to fizzle out of existence.

But there was one group of people who certainly didn't lose interest in me when I was leaving Japan, nor for some time afterwards: the bureaucrats. My departure triggered a final surge of forms and documentation from their arcane departments, and failure to cooperate with them would again come at a high price. For example, my pension contributions couldn't be returned unless I could prove that I had left Japan. A boarding card wouldn't suffice for this: only a photocopy of the stamp in my passport marked "Departed, Narita", with the date clearly visible, would do. Also, before they would reimburse my flight ticket back to London, they wanted a written estimate of the cost from the airline. When I asked them why they couldn't just call the airline for this information, they replied that all such estimates required certificates, and that all such certificates had to be duly stamped and dated.

I obtained the written estimate as requested, together with an appropriate certificate from the airline to testify that the estimate was genuine. But unfortunately matters didn't end there. The airline had added a rider to its "certificate" (which was, perhaps appropriately, presented to me with the words "Have a good fright!") that no estimate of fares to London could be guaranteed, because the price of a ticket could change at any time before it was actually issued. This declaration on the certificate that the estimate was an

estimate caused much disquiet and further bureaucratic zeal.
A ticket, the administrators insisted, couldn't be authorized
without the estimate; but the estimate would be worthless
if it were merely an estimate. To my unpractised eye this
seemed like an impasse beyond navigation. But they had
a brainwave: I could get the estimate of the ticket *and* the
actual ticket at the same time, thus guaranteeing the accuracy
of the estimate. This ingenious solution was relayed to me
by a former colleague in the following email, where the
idea of simultaneity is discreetly placed between brackets,
presumably to prevent either side losing face:

> *Dear Simon*
>
> *How are you? Are you enjoying excellent Spring days
> in Kamakura?*
>
> *The Faculty Office now require you to give a letter of
> estimate concerning the price of your one-way flight ticket
> before (or at the same time with) giving the receipt of the
> ticket. If you would give the estimate (and the receipt,
> hopefully) on 21 March, I would be very much pleased.*

So in the end I was able to leave the country in a manner
that satisfied the bureaucrats' requirements, naively assuming
that I had seen the back of them.

My naivety was short-lived. There were more pointless
ordeals to endure. A few days after my return to England,
they asked me for proof that I had not merely left Tokyo
on the 12.55 flight from Tokyo to London, but that I had
definitely landed in London. Without that confirmation,
neither my air fare, nor my other moving expenses, nor my
pension contributions could be refunded.

I immediately mailed Tokyo University a photocopy
of my boarding pass, which clearly showed the destination

of the flight as being London and the origin of the flight as being Tokyo, as well as a copy of the exit stamp in my passport. This surely suggested that I had been on a flight to London. Furthermore, by posting that photocopy I was proving that in the course of the flight I had not been jettisoned into the sea nor otherwise terminated, but had successfully reached London – otherwise how would I have been able to send a letter postmarked "London WC1"? But they still harboured doubts.

> *Dear Simon*
>
> *I certainly received your normal mail with the photocopy of your passport yesterday. Thank you very much for your quick treatment. However, the Faculty office says that photocopies of your passport to prove not only your departure from Narita but also your immigration at London is needed, because those photocopies must be the basis to pay your flight fee from Narita to London. Namely, they ask you to also send a photocopy of stamps of Heathrow to prove your arrival at London.*
>
> *They say that sending it by Fax would be OK if printing is clear. Anyway, would you please send it by either normal mail or fax? I really hope that you would grasp their inclination and understand their requirement.*
>
> *I wish you fruitful days in London, hoping to hear from you.*

After fulminating for twenty-four hours, I drafted a reply saying that nationals never "immigrate" back to their own countries. The very idea was oxymoronic – actually, just moronic. A moment's thought, however, reminded me that an argument of principle can always be disputed, and might even find an exception somewhere in the world

– such as, for example, Japan. And after all, despite the existence of a boarding pass and an exit stamp, it wasn't *technically* impossible that for some inexplicable reason I'd dashed off the plane just as the doors were about to close, jumped the security barriers, run the wrong way through passport control, been arrested and ended up in a Japanese jail.

So I decided to invoke the only sort of power the officials at Todai would understand: namely an insuperable bureaucratic impediment. I drafted a letter saying that I might have been able to ask the officials at Heathrow to stamp my passport if Tokyo University had provided me with a written request to this effect in advance of my arrival in London, but that it wasn't – administratively speaking – correct form to go back to the airport and ask Immigration for a retrospective stamp: they would not only refuse it, but might suspect the motives for requesting it and so launch an inquiry of their own, which would involve Tokyo University's administrators in a lot of extra work. I was tempted to point out, too, that having taken a London-bound flight which had not crashed, been hijacked or otherwise come to grief, I *must* have arrived in London. In the end, however, I abandoned all such convoluted arguments and sent back the following email:

> Dear Y***
>
> I cannot send you any stamps from the Immigration at London to prove my arrival, because the UK immigration authorities NEVER stamp the passports of arriving UK citizens (or, in fact, of any citizens from any country of the European Union, like France or Germany). You just show your passport and go through passport control. The Faculty Office should have told me in advance that they need that

*stamp and I could have asked for it. But they clearly said
that they only needed proof of leaving Narita. So what
can we do?*

*One suggestion to prove that I actually went to London
is that, on the next day, Saturday 7th, I flew from Heathrow
to Berlin and I still have my boarding card to prove that I
took that flight. Is that good enough?*

Best regards,

Simon

My patient former colleague, caught in the middle,
conceded the point:

Dear Simon

*Thank you for your message. I perfectly understand
your situation.*

*I will tell the Faculty Office about it next Monday. I
think this is not so serious issue, because you are actually
in London now, which would be logically impossible
without your arriving in London! This is almost a kind of
mathematical truth.*

*Anyway, I will tell you the result afterwards. Please
have a nice weekend.*

On the Monday the bureaucrats duly caved in. This, I am
sure, had nothing to do with the mathematical truth and
everything to do with the impossibility of getting fellow
bureaucrats at Heathrow airport to make an exception
to hallowed procedures by providing an entry permit to
someone who both didn't need it and had already entered the country. So reality was quietly acknowledged and
the matter swiftly dropped. Which confirms the ultimate
pragmatism of the Japanese when their ambitions turn out to

be undeniably impractical. My former colleague, evidently relieved, relayed the bureaucrats' surrender notice:

> *Dear Simon*
>
> *I told the Faculty Office today that British citizens do not have stamps made on the passport at airports when returning back to UK from foreign countries. They clearly understood, and said to me that it is OK to present only the photocopy of a stamp of Narita when you left Japan. Consequently, all issues would be done. I am really very happy, and guess that you might be in the same feeling as mine.*
>
> *Anyway, I am looking forward to seeing you in the near future, wishing you delightful Spring days in England.*

"All issues would be done"? It was an empty claim. There was another minor matter outstanding: my salary. This tricky topic had been under discussion for over one and a half years – in other words from seven months before I went to Japan and for a month after finally returning. The source of the stalemate was that my Oxford B.A. degree certificate had been issued more than a year after I had passed my final examinations – not an unusual procedure at Oxford, especially if, like me, new graduates delay attending degree ceremonies. Since pay at Tokyo University was primarily determined by how many years had elapsed since you formally graduated, rather than by anything so irrelevant as your track record as a teacher or writer, they couldn't decide whether my date of graduation was when I had passed the exams or when I had received the certificate. As a result, I had completed my year in Tokyo and left Japan without my precise salary ever being settled. Now they needed further emails from me explaining, yet again, the reasons for the discrepancy, so that they could retrospectively pay me my full entitlement. Though I'd always accepted that prevarication can be the very essence of decision-making, this seemed to take the principle one step too far, and to this day I have never been notified about whether the question of my salary at Todai has been formally resolved.

There couldn't have been a starker contrast between the bureaucrats' insatiable appetite for empty procedure and their casualness over a vital educational matter only a few weeks beforehand. The university examinations were to take place, and I had been sent the forms for recording my students' year-end exam and dissertation results. Examination results are central to the reputation of a university and, one would think, to the fortunes of its students. But these forms were hopelessly vague and lacked any clear standards for setting or marking papers. The setting of papers – their length, difficulty and precise subject matter – was entirely up to the professors who had taught the courses concerned. There was no coordination at all with other professors teaching closely related subjects. And the idea of having undergraduate finals or graduate dissertations marked by independent external examiners, or at least by two separate faculty members, which is standard practice at the best Western universities, was unheard of. In fact, when I was handed the forms, I was told that graduate students in our department were never failed. Among the 100% who were passed, there were two grades: "good" and "excellent". Most were deemed "excellent" – the University's highest accolade.

Undergraduates didn't have it too much harder. My straw poll of fellow professors suggested that a whopping 60% of students got "excellent", another 30% were classified "good", while only 5 to 10% got the next grade down, a "pass". Less than 5%, and often none, were failed; and the lowest grade of all, "bad fail", was never used. In order to fail, a student would need to know less about their subject than when they first entered the university – a perfectly achievable objective, given what anyone can forget if they take a four-year vacation. But such students would generally be marked "unclassified", which meant that they had attended classes too seldom to be evaluated, or else that they had completely failed to take the exams or produce their dissertations.

Todai, among the hardest to enter of the world's universities, must therefore be one of the very easiest to leave. The nail-biting, life-determining months of "examination hell", or *shiken-jigoku*, that decide admission to Japan's great universities are balanced by what can only be called the "examination heaven" that paves the way to graduation. Though failure to be admitted has triggered many a suicide, failure to graduate with high marks barely registers, except with particularly ambitious parents or those set on legal or bureaucratic careers. The least concerned of all are the great corporations, which have long disregarded the graduation results of most Japanese universities, taking all but the most rigorous technical qualifications with a very large pinch of salt. Indeed, the corporations are the *real* universities in Japan, the places where all those superbly trained engineers and technologists and managers come into their own.

If I think back over my year at Todai, still Japan's most famous university, I feel an acute sense of sadness about the place and the way it symbolizes all that is wrong with the Japanese way. So much talent, so many resources, such opportunities – wasted. Apart from the bureaucrats, some of my colleagues and a handful of students, almost everyone I met seemed semi-detached, at best. Most undergraduates were mentally on permanent vacation. The Dean and his staff seemed preoccupied with implementing the rules and protecting their perks. I was never informed of the syllabus – perhaps there was no syllabus to inform me of. I was never asked what precisely I would be teaching my students; as far as the administrators were concerned, I could have been lecturing on the adventures of Peter Rabbit or reading a comic out loud.

But, as I set out for Narita airport – exactly one year to the day since I had arrived – I felt that this unceremonious ending to my stay in this extraordinarily ceremonious country, this petering out of so many relationships amid such bureaucratic absurdity, had a point. Though I no longer possessed an official position in Japanese society, and so in a sense no longer existed, Japan had grown so deeply into me that any formal ending would have been contrived and unreal. And the nation posed inescapable riddles that no leaving ceremony could exorcize: not only riddles about what Japan was and would become, but also, more pressingly for me, a challenge to many of my own, typically Western, assumptions. Such as: Is the core of love really everlasting? How important are truth and truthfulness – to our relationships, to social cohesion, to our maturation as individuals? Has the cult of sincerity in the West become a front for *playing* at openness, even for lies and deception? Is much self-knowledge possible if, as seems likely, we have no stable, continuous self to know, no inner core that remains untouched by our constantly changing social roles and environments? What are the limits of real compassion, which in Japan seldom extend beyond relationships that one feels actively involved in? When is pity merely a pretext for controlling others or, indeed, for *refusing* to see their real suffering? Is marriage conducive to love? Or should we accept reality and allow people to express their love for others without sacrificing their marriages? Must things we value be permanent?

Many, many more questions about my own preconceptions were forced on me by this ultimately pragmatic, yet very romantic nation that, unlike the Western tradition, does not necessarily regard truth as supremely important, or pity as the core of morality, or individual life as priceless, or eternity as found in a grain of sand, or even good as absolutely distinct from bad. Japan is stubborn proof that we inhabit a world where people can hold thoroughly un-Western values and yet have a deeply successful, resilient and, in different ways, humane culture – stubborn proof that the whole industrialized world might not, after all, be converging on Anglo-Saxon values.

Oddly, about Japan itself I had fewer doubts. I left feeling profoundly confident in the Japanese people's extraordinary ability to emerge with renewed vigour from their crises, whether economic or social or spiritual or political or – as at the dawn of the new millennium – all of these. Sufficient reforms might well be delayed until the eleventh hour, or even until a catastrophic collapse, because of the national devotion to consensus, to secrecy, and to an absurd bureaucratization of almost every aspect of life. These ills have fostered corruption, inefficiency, dishonesty, destruction of the natural environment, useless "public works", appalling architecture and inadequate higher education. But a new, stronger Japan will emerge, thanks to its people's immense resilience, patience, skills, love of precision, sound judgement, and – ultimately – realism and adaptability. The Japanese have after all changed more radically and more often since the nineteenth century than perhaps any other nation in the world. They have been able to live with a thoroughly hybrid culture of traditional and

Western influences without anything like the social and emotional upheaval that modernization has unleashed in countries as diverse as France and China, Spain and Iran, Argentina and Germany. As with individuals, however, so with nations: everything depends on Japan's continued will to live, its determination to prevail, its love of the future, its ability to harness the strengths of its heritage to the demands and opportunities of the present. And about that, only time will tell – though I remain firmly on the side of the optimists.

ABOUT THE AUTHOR

Dr Simon May is Fellow in Philosophy at Birkbeck College, University of London. His writings draw not only on his wide philosophical learning, but also on his experience outside academia, in international politics and business. Dr May has been a close adviser to various world statesmen, held senior positions in the European Union, and served on the Board of Directors of both public and private companies. His most recent books are *The Little Book of Big Thoughts* (2005), a collection of his own aphorisms, and *Nietzsche's Ethics and his War on "Morality"* (2002). He lives in London.